PHILIP ALLAN

Philip Allan Updates, an imprint of Hodder Education, an Hachette UK company, Market Place, Deddington, Oxfordshire OX15 0SE

Orders
Bookpoint Ltd, 130 Milton Park, Abingdon, Oxfordshire, OX14 4SB
tel: 01235 827827
fax: 01235 400401
e-mail: education@bookpoint.co.uk
Lines are open 9.00 a.m.–5.00 p.m., Monday to Saturday, with a 24-hour message answering service. You can also order through the Philip Allan Updates website: www.philipallan.co.uk

ISBN 978-1-4441-4785-8

First printed 2011
Impression number 6 5 4 3 2 1
Year 2014 2013 2012 2011

Printed in Italy

Hachette UK's policy is to use papers that are natural, renewable and recyclable products and made from wood grown in sustainable forests. The logging and manufacturing processes are expected to conform to the environmental regulations of the country of origin.

P01921

Contents

Introduction

Content Guidance

Questions & Answers

Getting the most from this book

Questions & Answers

Exam-style questions

Examiner comments on the questions
Tips on what you need to do to gain full marks, indicated by the icon 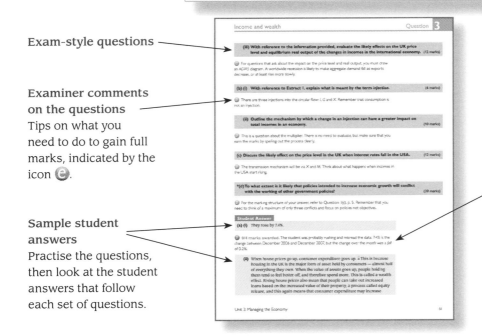.

Sample student answers
Practise the questions, then look at the student answers that follow each set of questions.

Examiner commentary on sample student answers
Find out how many marks each answer would be awarded in the exam and then read the examiner comments (preceded by the icon ⓔ) following each student answer. Annotations that link back to points made in the student answers show exactly how and where marks are gained or lost.

How to use this book

This guide has been written to prepare students for Unit 2 of Edexcel's Advanced Subsidiary (AS) GCE examinations in economics. It provides an overview of the knowledge and skills required to achieve a high grade in the examination for 'Managing the Economy'. The unit's main emphasis is on the issues associated with measures of economic performance, income and wealth, aggregate demand and supply, and macroeconomic policy in the UK:

(1) Measuring the performance of countries. As an introduction to economics, we look at a range of ways in which we can assess the economic performance of a country. Economics is a study of the management of resources, and *macroeconomics* looks at indicators at an aggregate or total level. For example, in Unit 2 we do not look at the individual pricing decisions of a firm or consumer, but at all the prices in the economy. We do not focus on whether one person's wage will make him or her unemployable, but consider wages and employment levels throughout the economy.

(2) Income and wealth. In this section we introduce a simple way of understanding the macroeconomy: as a circular flow of income. The causal relationships between income and spending, spending and output, and output and income make up the circle. In this context we can understand how injections and leakages will alter the flow and have a significant macroeconomic impact.

(3) Aggregate demand and supply. These are the forces which together determine the price level and equilibrium real output in the economy. We examine what causes these to shift and the likely impact on the macroeconomy.

(4) Economic growth — causes, constraints and costs. Using aggregate demand and supply analysis, we can give reasons for changes in the rate of economic growth, and indicate some of the likely side-effects.

(5) Macroeconomic objectives of governments. This section brings the government into the picture of how the economy functions.

(6) Policy instruments. The tools that the government uses to try to influence the macro-economy are explained, and their functions and likely side-effects are examined. It becomes apparent that in trying to improve some aspects of the economy, other aspects are also affected, sometimes for the better but often for the worse.

This guide is aimed at developing your AS skills, and should be used alongside your notes and other revision aids. The guide includes typical questions and answers, and explains what the examiners are looking for. Common mistakes are highlighted and several strategies for increasing your marks are suggested.

The Content Guidance section provides an overview of the main topics, identifying what has to be learnt and explaining the theoretical requirements of the unit.

The final part of the guide provides questions and answers on the economic concepts and topics in Unit 2 with explanation of the exam format and the skills that will be tested. There are four data-response questions covering the main topic areas, with a selection of student answers to give you an idea of the level of answer required to achieve a grade A. The answers are interspersed with examiner's comments — a helpful way of getting to know the expectations of those who will mark your papers. After reviewing the Unit 2 topics, you should try these sample questions, ideally under timed conditions, and then compare your work with the answers and comments provided. This will allow you to identify areas of weakness that require further work.

Content guidance

This section focuses on the **macroeconomic** concepts and models that students need to understand for Unit 2: Managing the Economy. The information is organised under the following headings:

- Measurements of economic performance
- Income flows and wealth effects
- Aggregate demand and supply
- Economic growth — causes, constraints and costs
- Macroeconomic objectives of governments
- Policy instruments

Measurements of economic performance

Economic growth

There are two meanings of the term **economic growth**: **actual growth** is an increase in real incomes or **gross domestic product (GDP)**; and **potential growth** is an increase in the productive capacity in a country.

If economic growth is measured using national income, then the value is meaningless unless the figures are given in real rather than nominal terms. Real values have been adjusted to remove the effects of inflation, whereas nominal values are the current incomes that you would see if they were unadjusted.

Furthermore, for GDP to have any significance in terms of standards of living, figures must be given per head (or 'per capita'). If a country's income increases by 10% but the population increases by 20%, people are actually worse off per head.

Another important distinction required when measuring economic growth is to look at *values* rather than *volumes*. Firms might achieve higher sales figures because they sell more in volume or number of products, but if those sales are worth less per unit then they are not in fact seeing an increase in the value of their output. As an example, consider Germany and China. Germany is the biggest exporter in the world by *value*, whereas China exports much more in terms of *volume* of goods.

How is GDP measured?

Gross domestic product is the sum of all goods and services produced in a country in a year. It is also the sum of all incomes earned in a year, and the sum of all expenditure in one country in a year. Consider it as a circular flow of income where for everything that is earned, something must be produced and something must be

Knowledge check 1

Why is economic growth not the same as GDP?

Examiner tip

Real values have the effects of inflation removed. If inflation is 2% and your wage rise is 2% then your real wages do not rise at all.

Examiner tip

GDP is best measured in real terms, per capita (or per head)

Knowledge check 2

What is the difference between constant prices (or real) GDP and current (or nominal) GDP?

spent. The government measures all three flows: goods, income and expenditure, which in theory should amount to the same figure (currently around £1.4 trillion in the UK). However, in practice, errors and omissions mean that there are some discrepancies.

Increases in GDP are therefore a sign that a country is experiencing increasing incomes, output and spending. On the face of it, this is a good thing because people can have more goods and services, implying that they have a better standard of living. However, there are many reasons why this might not be the case. If I earn more, it may be that I work longer hours and have more work pressures, or that I have a higher cost of living, such as increased mortgage payments. Pollution is likely to increase as I travel more miles, and there is a whole range of social costs that may be incurred.

Problems of comparison

Let's say that economic growth is 10% in China, 6% in Bangladesh and around 2% in the UK. These figures may mask several differences not accounted for in GDP statistics:

- **Subsistence, barter and the black economy.** If farmers consume their own output, if goods are traded without the price system (e.g. by barter), or if goods are paid for without being declared for tax purposes, then national income will not reflect the true standard of living. Estimates of the size of the hidden economy are UK 7%, Italy 30%, Russia 50% and sub-Saharan Africa up to 60%.
- **Currency values.** When trying to compare countries, there is a difficulty in knowing whether to use the official value of a currency or the purchasing power of that currency. This is discussed in the section on the Human Development Index, pp. 16–17.
- **Income distribution.** When comparing countries' income per head, some sense of the income distribution should also be taken into account. In some cases, a large proportion of income is earned by a very few, which makes the mean income much higher than the income enjoyed by the ordinary person. In this way, the general standard of living in a country can appear higher than it really is for most people.
- **Size of the public sector.** If much of the spending in the economy is by government, it might or might not improve welfare for the population. The public sector is the part of the economy controlled by the government. It is around 50% of the UK economy but in developing countries it is usually significantly less than 20%.
- **Consumer and capital spending.** Spending on investment goods might mean standard of living increases in the future, but at the expense of living standards today. It is better to take account of future growth patterns rather than simply considering today's income, and stark economic growth figures should be broken down to look at the investment element.
- **Quality issues.** Spending on schools might be high, for example, but how can we measure quality? Are improving results enough to prove that living standards are rising?

These problems in comparing GDP figures between countries and over time mean that comparisons of living standards are likely to be inaccurate if they are based solely on GDP. However, real income growth per head is a good guide to actual growth

Examiner tip

Standards of living include factors besides economic growth, although economic growth has a part to play in increasing living standards if the increased incomes are spread out across the economy.

Examiner tip

The rate of increase in GDP in real terms is known as **actual** economic growth. It means there is more spending, higher incomes and higher output in the economy.

if these other factors can be taken into account. The rate of increase in productive possibilities is the rate of potential economic growth. There is more capacity in the economy, which might be because the labour supply has increased, there has been investment, or productivity has increased. It can be used to show how an economy is performing relative to its output capacity. Differences between the two are known as the output gap. Although a more useful measure, potential economic growth is hard to measure accurately. See shifts in *AD* and *AS* on p. 26 and output gaps on p. 28.

Knowledge check 3

Why do developing countries tend to have higher growth rates than developed ones?

Links and common themes

- The issues of the external costs of increased economic growth are discussed in Unit 1. You do not need to know the externalities diagram for Unit 2, but the concept of spillover effects is the same.
- Both an increase in aggregate demand and an increase in aggregate supply may increase the rate of growth in an economy, but not always. (See the section on economic growth, pp. 28–31.)
- Growth can increase living standards, but policies to increase growth might worsen the environment or widen income gaps. (See the section on macroeconomic policy conflicts, pp. 34–36.)
- Growth is a necessary but not sufficient condition to relieve poverty in developing countries. This is a topic you are likely to discuss in Unit 4: The Global Economy.

Inflation

Inflation is a sustained rise in the general price level. The general price level is measured using an index such as the **consumer prices index (CPI)**. The reason for using an index is that percentage changes can be shown easily, and it makes effective comparisons possible.

Two surveys need to be undertaken. One is to collect information about what people buy, currently known as the expenditure and food survey. This involves collecting information from a sample of nearly 7,000 households in the UK using self-reported diaries of all purchases, including food eaten out. The proportion of income spent on each item is used to ascertain weighting. For example, if 10% is spent on food, then 10% of the weighting is assigned to food.

The second survey is of prices. The price survey is undertaken by civil servants who collect data once a month about changes in the price of the 650 most commonly used goods and services in a variety of retail outlets. Because similar items can be bought in high- and low-cost shops, a selection of prices is gathered for each item, with 120,000 prices gathered in all. The price changes are multiplied by the weights to give a price index; you can measure inflation from this by calculating the percentage change in this index over consecutive years.

Assessing the measure of inflation

Since December 2003, the UK government's target for CPI inflation has been 2% (±1%). This means that small price rises are acceptable to the UK government. If prices rise by more than 3% they become a concern, but if they begin to rise by less than 1%, or even fall, then risks of deflation and even a recession might arise.

Examiner tip

Inflation is a general and sustained increase in prices, measured by a change in a weighted index of prices such as the CPI.

Knowledge check 4

Why is an index used?

Examiner tip

CPI measures price levels, not the level of inflation — unless you are given 'CPI inflation', which means inflation as measured using the CPI.

Knowledge check 5

Why are there two surveys for the CPI?

Knowledge check 6

Is it true to say that measures such as the CPI are described as 'excluding mortgages'?

Knowledge check 7

Why does the government like to exclude housing costs in the main measure of inflation?

Knowledge check 8

Although you may be able to explain the distinction between the two types of inflation measure, can you explain how one measure can rise while the other falls, or why they might come closer together or move further apart?

Examiner tip

Don't confuse price levels (e.g. CPI) with rates of inflation. Increases in CPI are inflation. The rate of inflation may fall even when price levels are still rising. If inflation is above zero but falling then the price level is rising at a slower rate.

Knowledge check 9

How is inflation measured? Clue: many students waste a lot of time by saying what inflation is. Instead talk about the two surveys.

One problem with the CPI measure is that it does not include housing costs such as mortgage interest repayments or rent. Monthly mortgage payments often form a large part of a household's spending and are certainly a cost of living for almost 10 million households in the UK, with an average mortgage debt of £130,000. So if the CPI rises by only 2% and inflation seems to be under control, a rise in interest rates means that many households will nevertheless be experiencing the effect of higher mortgage payments.

For many people, wage increases are linked to the rate of inflation, and if the CPI measure is used, wage increases will fail to take into account a large part of household expenditure in the form of housing costs. A more appropriate measure for wage increases is the **retail price index (RPI)**. This is more inclusive than the CPI, but it is not as reliable for international comparisons and the statistical method of basing the data is also unique to the UK. Moreover, because the RPI includes the cost of mortgage interest repayments and these will rise when interest rates are raised, any interest rate rise implemented to tackle inflation will have a one-off effect of making inflation appear worse, which makes the policy-makers look incompetent.

There are several other problems with the CPI measure:

- CPI measures the cost of living only for an *average* household. The top and bottom 4% income brackets are not included; nor are pensioners.
- There are sampling problems: only 57% of households respond to the survey, and when they do respond they might not give accurate information about recent spending of various members within the household.
- The 650 items in the 'basket' are changed only once a year, but tastes and fashions change more quickly than this. In addition, the basket does not reflect the fact that changes in retail outlets such as 'buy one, get one free' temporarily change people's spending habits.
- For people with atypical spending patterns, such as vegetarians and non-drivers, the CPI will be unrepresentative. For example, those who often buy rail tickets will experience inflation well above 2%.
- When the quality of goods changes, the measure breaks down because it is not comparing like with like. If I bought a more expensive mobile phone this year than last year, the price change might not be the result of inflation but because I wanted an upgrade.

Useful exercises

- Visit **www.statistics.gov.uk** and calculate your own rate of inflation using the 'personal inflation calculator' (type these words into the site's main search engine). Then imagine you are your granny and do the same. Do you think incomes for students and pensioners should be linked to a measure of inflation more reflective of both your spending patterns?
- Visit the Bank of England website, to see the current rate of inflation, the current rate of interest and recent inflation reports. Alternatively, if you live near London, visit the Bank of England museum in Threadneedle Street. Entry is free.

Employment and unemployment

The **level of employment** is the number of people in work, while the **rate of employment** is the proportion of people in work relative to the size of the workforce. The **workforce** consists of those people who are at work or those of working age who are willing and able to work (i.e. the employed *and* the unemployed).

The **unemployed** are people who are willing and available to work, but are not currently employed. The **level of unemployment** is the number out of work, and the **rate of unemployment** gives this figure as a proportion of the workforce.

Factors that influence levels of employment

Employment is affected by the following factors:
- **The school leaving age.** This is rising to 18 by 2015. Employment in the age range 16–18 will fall but in the longer term it will make school leavers more employable.
- **Number of school leavers entering higher or further education.** Although over 40% of students now carry on in education after 18 in the UK, this is likely to fall now that many students have to pay over £9,000 a year in university fees.
- **Level of net migration.** Net migration is the difference between those coming into the country (immigration) and those leaving (emigration). Most immigrants into the UK come to study (37%), but the second most common reason is related to work (34%). This figure has fallen since a major influx in 2004 when ten new countries joined the EU, with their inhabitants enjoying full rights to enter the UK for work. Immigration is likely to increase both employment and unemployment.
- **Availability of jobs.** There are likely to be higher levels of employment if there are more jobs available.
- **Level of taxes and benefits.** If taxes on income are high, or out-of-work benefits are generous, then there is a disincentive for people to work.

Knowledge check 10

Why does an increase in immigration lead to an increase in employment and unemployment?

There are two main ways of measuring unemployment. The International Labour Organisation uses the **Labour Force Survey**, which is now the official measure used in the UK. This involves a face-to-face interview followed by a quarterly telephone survey of 60,000 households, asking several questions including whether anyone in the household has been out of work for 4 weeks and is ready to start in the next 2 weeks. The questions relate to anyone over the age of 16, and it is therefore a more inclusive survey than the claimant count (see below). However, the survey data are 6 weeks out of date by the time they are published, which happens every month.

The **claimant count** is a measure of unemployment which records the number of people who are claiming jobseeker's allowance (JSA). There is some stigma attached to claiming benefits, so not everyone who is eligible to claim does so, and many are not eligible because the criteria for eligibility are very tight. For example, if you have resigned from your previous job within the last 6 months, or have refused three jobs that you have been offered, then you cannot claim.

In order to gain the full benefit of around £65 a week, you need to have made a certain number of National Insurance Contributions by working in the past. You also have to prove, in an interview at the job centre every 2 weeks, that you are looking for work. Under the rules of the New Deal, you might be denied benefits unless you actively

involve yourself in training or work placements. After 6 months of claiming JSA you will be means tested, and claims are substantially reduced if you have a partner who earns or if you have savings above £8,000; payments are stopped altogether if you have more than £16,000. You must be over 18 and below retirement age (although the rate of JSA is significantly lower for those aged 18 to 25 than for those over 25). If you are unable to work, or are working in a voluntary capacity for more than 16 hours a week, you cannot claim.

The claimant count therefore does not present the full picture of unemployment. It is quick and cheap to obtain these data, however, and it is a useful measure of hardship — after all, you are not very likely to claim jobseeker's allowance if you don't need the money between jobs.

Knowledge check 11

Is the claimant count the measure of those eligible to receive JSA or the number receiving it?

Useful exercises

- Visit **www.statistics.gov.uk** and in the 'Economy' section search for the questions asked in the Labour Force Survey. Consider reasons why the data that the answers produce might be unreliable.
- One explanation for the relative changes in the Labour Force Survey and the claimant count is the stage of the economic cycle. List two reasons why this might be so and check them with your teacher or the 'Labour market' section of the **www.statistics.gov.uk** website.
- Look up the JSA on **www.direct.gov.uk** to find out all the eligibility criteria, current rates and more. You need to search the site for jobseeker's allowance.

Knowledge check 12

Look at the latest data on employment and unemployment on the **www.statistics.gov.uk** website (go to 'UK snapshot' then choose 'Labour market'). If you add together employment and unemployment in the UK, you will reach a figure of around 80%. What are the other 20% doing?

Links and common themes

- When there are unemployed resources such as labour, the economy is operating inside its production possibility frontier (see Unit 1).
- Spare capacity is also a sign that there is an output gap, which is equivalent to the relatively elastic part of the aggregate supply curve, discussed on pp. 24–27.
- Inflation can redistribute incomes (e.g. from savers to borrowers), and some analysts believe that tolerating inflation means that lower levels of unemployment can be enjoyed. However, inflation makes a country less competitive if its inflation rate is higher than those of its main trading partners. This could mean that a current account deficit develops or that the exchange rate falls, which is even more inflationary. These conflicts and compounding problems are discussed in the section on 'Conflicts between objectives', pp. 34–36.

Types and costs of unemployment

There are two very different views on unemployment. On one side, in the 'classical view', there are only unemployed people who are not able and willing to work at the going wage rate. In other words, if people would accept a lower wage they could find jobs. In this view all unemployment is therefore just a short-term problem and the best solution is 'laissez faire' — that is, leave the market to get on with it, and eventually the problem of unemployment will go away.

If people accept lower wages then the costs of living will fall as firms do not need to charge such high prices, so in fact workers will find the lower wages are acceptable once they start working. For this reason it is also called 'real wage' unemployment, where wages have been forced above the market-clearing wage. People who believe that this is the only cause of unemployment think that out-of-work benefits should be cut, trade unions should be curtailed and there should not be a minimum wage. Thus, unemployed people will be forced to work.

In the opposing, 'Keynesian' view, people can be unemployed even in the long run. This is because there is insufficient aggregate demand in the economy. If you agree that the economy can be in equilibrium but not everyone has a job then you are arguing that there is **demand deficient** unemployment or **cyclical unemployment**. Keynes said that if people do not spend, and save too much, then there are multiplier effects in the economy, and less spending means there are fewer job opportunities. If people are losing jobs then there will be even less spending and so the vicious circle continues. Even if wages are cut there will not be more people employed — in fact lower wages will mean that there is even less spending, so even fewer people are needed in employment.

Apart from saving too much, other reasons for demand deficient unemployment are lack of business confidence; and increase in the value of a currency; slow rates of productivity growth relative to other countries; external shocks such as oil price rises (oil is imported and demand is price inelastic, so if prices rise there will be less spending in the UK); and increased use of imports from low wage economies.

Another argument for employment problems that are not linked solely to labour being unwilling to work at the going rate is that the economy is undergoing structural change, and therefore different types of labour are required. The skill set of those, for example, who are trained in manufacturing will not have much value in a business based in the service sector. Clearly, over time, as fewer people are being trained for manufacturing and more for services, this kind of **structural unemployment** will disappear. But as Keynes said, 'in the long run we are all dead', so in the view of many there ought to be proactive policies put in place to deal with both demand-deficient and structural kinds of unemployment.

There will always be **frictional unemployment** — that is, people who are moving from one job to another — but this kind of unemployment is a sign of a healthy, flexible labour market with people willing to change jobs in order to improve their prospects.

Costs of unemployment

The costs of unemployment to the economy include:
- **The cost to the individual and dependants.** People will have lower incomes and living standards will fall. However, there is a wider unseen cost, as people out of work lose morale and their skill sets can become quickly obsolete.
- **The cost to firms.** Firms will find that people spend less, so they will have to lower prices and will make less profit. However, it may mean that people are more willing to stay in their jobs owing to fear of unemployment, so they may be willing to work harder.
- **The cost to government.** As unemployment rises the government has to pay more in jobseekers' benefits and will receive less in tax.

Knowledge check 13

What is the difference between an employment rate and an employment level?

Summary

- Employment is just over 29 million, meaning that in the UK almost one in every two people in the population works. The employment rate — the percentage of workers relative to the number of working age — is in the range of 70–80% in the UK.
- High levels of employment have benefits for the workers (higher incomes and the human capital factor – when you work you gain or retain skills in industry), governments (lower payments of JSA,

higher levels of tax receipts), and firms (higher levels of spending with multiplier effects). There are said to be improved social effects when people are busy.
- Unemployment in the UK reached 8% after the 2008–10 recession, although in many countries it was much higher. The remaining people of working age who are neither employed nor unemployed are either unwilling or unable to take on full-time work (students, houseworkers or people caring for family).

Current account of the balance of payments

The **balance of payments** is a record of payments between one country and the rest of the world. The most significant element of it for your AS exam is the **current account**, which records trade in goods, trade in services, investment income and transfers. A country such as Germany, which exports a large number of high-value goods, has a **surplus** on the current account, meaning that more money flows in (for the purchase of German goods and services by foreigners) than flows out for imports. On the other hand, a country that enjoys a high living standard and a high level of confidence, and which is not as successful in export markets, is likely to be running a current account **deficit** where outflows are greater than inflows. Examples are the USA, Spain and the UK.

On its own, a balance of payments deficit on the current account is not a problem for an economy as long as it can be funded, but it becomes a problem as reserves of foreign currencies begin to run low. It might mean that the currency falls in value, which is inflationary (imports become more expensive). It might be a sign that the country is becoming uncompetitive (costs rising relative to trading partners) and might in the long run mean that a painful readjustment, such as tax increases, is required to stop people overspending.

Trade in goods measures the movement of tangible products across international borders. The UK is a large exporter of pharmaceuticals and cars, but a major importer of foodstuffs and, since 2005, a net importer of oil and gas. **Trade in services** measures movement of intangible output. The UK is a major exporter of banking and insurance services, but an importer of foreign holidays (because the British like to go abroad).

Investment income is a measure of interest, profit and dividends that are rewards for capital investments in another country. For example, if a British person buys shares in a US company, the shares will not appear on the current account, but any dividends will appear as a positive figure on the UK current account. Finally, **transfers** refer to the movement of funds for which there is no corresponding trade in goods and services. Examples are taxes paid to the EU, payments to British military personnel working in another country, and when economic migrants send some of their incomes back to their families in another country.

Examiner tip

There are four components of the current account of the balance of payments. If you disaggregate the figures, you will see that they are not all negative even if the overall balance is negative.

Causes and costs of an imbalance

The **cause** of a current account imbalance may be that a country is spending too much, or that it is not producing anything that potential customers abroad want to buy. It may be because of the stage in the business cycle, which clearly may be different for different countries at different times, or the strength of the currency. For example, if sterling is strong against the dollar, the UK is likely to export less and import more, because the price of UK exports rises relative to other products on the world market, and imports become relatively cheap in the UK. Perhaps the most significant factor in the UK is the loss of competitiveness in the manufacturing sector owing to higher costs of factors of production in the UK relative to the Far East. It takes time for economies to adjust to changing comparative costs, and during the adjustment process the UK is likely to face an ongoing deficit.

The **costs** of a current account imbalance become significant only when the deficit (or surplus) becomes unsustainable. **Sustainability** means that the needs of the present are met without compromising the ability of future generations to meet their own needs. Persistent deficits can make the value of a currency fall, so in some economies the government might try to buy up surplus currency in order to maintain its value. (This does not happen in the UK.) A fall in the value of the currency may restore competitiveness, as it makes imports seem more expensive and exports relatively cheap on international markets. Persistent deficits see net incomes leave the country, which might mean demand in the domestic country is subdued. If you are a worker you might lose your job, but from the perspective of the Monetary Policy Committee of the Bank of England, this might be a welcome development, preventing the onset of inflation.

Common examination errors

- One of the most common misunderstandings is the analysis of what happens to the current account of the balance of payments when the interest rate rises. This is only partially within the scope of this unit and will be discussed in detail in Unit 4, but it is important not to argue that 'hot money enters the country and this improves the balance' because hot money is not part of the current account. The best argument to pursue in Unit 2 is that when the interest rate rises, the exchange rate usually rises too, so exports will become less competitive and imports more so.

Knowledge check 14

Are your holidays abroad an 'import'?

Useful exercises

- On an internet search engine, type in 'UK balance of payments first release' with the current year to see a summary of the current account in recent years, with simple graphs.
- The 'Pink Book' (type 'Pink Book Balance of Payments' into an internet search engine) is more up-to-date and very detailed, but perhaps not so easy to interpret.

Examiner tip

If interest rates rise, the exchange rate is likely to rise. This makes exports relatively expensive, and imports relatively cheap, so it is likely to worsen the balance of payments in the long run.

Links and common themes

- Many students find the current account the most mystifying of all the measures of economic performance. This is partly because Unit 2 is a holistic study and you need to know the rest of the unit before this part fully makes sense. Furthermore, it is just a partial look at international trade, which will be covered in more depth in Unit 4.

Measures of development: the Human Development Index

Economic development measures the *quality* of growth, rather than merely an increase in incomes. In order to measure the quality of growth we may take into account access to resources, living standards, the ability to make choices and the sustainability of growth. Composite indicators such as the **Human Development Index (HDI)** have been developed by the United Nations to combine the advantages of GDP measures and non-GDP economic and social indicators.

The HDI is a measure of standards of living used since 1990 and has been updated in 2010. It comprises three equally weighted elements: one-third health (measured by life expectancy at birth), one-third years of schooling and one-third GDP per head at **purchasing power parity**. This means that the rate of conversion of the local currency into US dollars is such that the same basket of goods and services could be bought in each country.

There are two ways in which you might come across the Human Development Index. One is as a **rank**, where number 1 is the top and then countries get worse as the number rises. The other way is as an **index**, where the number 1 means the best and 0 is the worst. In an examination you are most likely to see the index, and you should know that 1 to 0.8 is considered to be a high level of human development, 0.8 to 0.5 is medium, and below 0.5 is low.

Assessing the HDI

The HDI is a helpful measure of development because it uses reliable and fairly easy-to-obtain indicators, takes income into account but qualifies income in terms of the cost of living. The figures chosen have been judged to be those that can be recorded with the most consistency. The method of measuring the HDI was updated by the UNDP in 2010, removing a literacy test and changing the statistical methods. In your exam, either the pre- or post-2010 method will be accepted in your answers.

However, the HDI has some problems: it gives no indication of the distribution of incomes, and an indication of deprivation might make it more useful. For example, the **Human Poverty Index** is an index developed in 1997 which records what people go without rather than what they have. This might be more useful for governments or donors. Life expectancy is easy to measure but it does not give any indication of the quality of life. Years of schooling might be unreliable if it means that students are repeating years because they cannot make progress, or if the teachers are themselves untrained, or if there is a high level of absenteeism — of students or teachers.

Examiner tip

The HDI has advantages, but you must also be aware of its limitations.

Edexcel AS Economics

Common examination errors

- A common mistake is to confuse ranks (where 1 is the highest, falling to 177, which is currently Zimbabwe) with index numbers (where 1 is perfect and 0 is where humans cannot live).

Useful exercises

- Visit the United Nations Development Programme website (**www.undp.org**) to see the latest Human Development Report. The tables in the back of the report give the GDP, HDI and other indicator ranks. These are also listed fairly accurately on Wikipedia.
- You can see the results of this exercise in the final column of Table 1 in the UN Human Development Report. The higher the figure, whether positive or negative, the greater the disparity between purely income measures and health and education measures of human development.

Links and common themes

- The concept of HDI is invaluable for assessing the performance of developing countries, and the knowledge acquired here is intended to prepare you for the work you will cover in Unit 4.

Other measures of development

There are many other ways to judge the development of a country. Each has its advantages and disadvantages, and a selection of indicators could be chosen to show changes over time or to compare changes in different countries.

One indicator which signifies not just standards of living but potential for development is the measure of **mobile phones per thousand of the population**. Mobile technology allows a catch of fish to be brought into a port where prices are highest, or can be used to develop a cashless trading system in a country where the currency and finance systems are insecure. Mobiles don't rely on a constant supply of electricity and are therefore a strong indication that a country can develop despite problems in infrastructure.

Another very helpful indicator is the **proportion of workers involved in agriculture**. In Asia and sub-Saharan Africa, around two-thirds of the workforce is employed in agriculture. In Latin America the proportion is around 25%, but in developed countries the figure is usually below 2%. The greater the proportion, the less likely it is that the country has high actual or potential growth. The marginal product of labour in agriculture is likely to be very low, and workers are likely to have little income and little access to other forms of work where incomes could rise. However, living in an agricultural environment does provide some protection from international shocks such as global recession, in that the produce can be life sustaining if not always income generating.

Knowledge check 15

Choose any country and find its GDP per head ranking at PPP values and its HDI. Subtract the second from the first. What does the sign mean?

Problems in using other measures of development

Many measures have data collection problems. Some data, such as disease indicators, are difficult to gain with accuracy because cause of death might not be known or might be concealed for cultural or political reasons.

Another problem is that indicators can overlap, so although a wider use of indicators might give a broader picture, it might also give a very uneven picture. For example, access to safe water and disease indicators are likely to be closely related, increasing the weight of the health measure relative to incomes and education.

Knowledge check 16

AIDS is a clear indicator that there is a problem with human development. Why do no indicators or measures include AIDS statistics?

Knowledge check 17

What is the main difference between economic growth and economic development?

Useful exercises

● Look at the latest Human Development Report at **www.undp.org** and choose a non-GDP-based indicator, such as newspapers bought per thousand. Think of a reason why it might be a good sign of development (in this case, literacy) and a poor indicator (it depends on the type of newspaper, or whether the press allows freedom of information).

Links and common themes

● Other measures of economic development include absolute and relative poverty. These will be studied in Unit 4.

Summary

● GDP is a measure of the value of output of goods and services in a country in a given period of time. Increases in GDP or increases in potential GDP are called economic growth. There are problems with the reliability of the measure, when comparing the performance of different economies and comparing an economy over time. However, the data we have are very useful when adjusted to real, per head values using an exchange rate weighted to reflect the cost of living in the country. Used with other indicators it helps economists to assess the standards of living in a country.

● There are two measures of unemployment, giving a broader picture of the problem of unused resources, but there are problems with measuring unemployment by both measures. The advantage of having two measures is that they can cancel out each other's deficiencies.

● Inflation is a measure of the general rise in the price level. It is measured using two surveys. One is based on consumer expenditure, finding out how much people spend on the things they buy over a period of time: that is, their 'basket of goods'. Weights are attached to each item to represent the proportion spent on each item. These weights are then multiplied

by the price changes, which are collected in a separate survey known as the 'price survey'. The weights are divided out of the final figure to give a weighted measure of the new price level. The most commonly used measures in the UK are the RPI (including housing costs) and CPI (excluding housing costs).

● The balance of payments records international payments between one country and the rest of the world. The current account of the balance of payments records transactions that are income for the recipient, rather than investments or loans. There are four elements in the current account: trade in goods, trade in services, investment income and transfer payments.

● The Human Development Index is a composite measure of economic development, which combines three factors chosen to represent the broad areas of income, health and education. There are many other ways to measure economic development, and each has its own advantages and disadvantages. Economic development is a broad concept, and therefore there is a broad range of ways to measure it. Real income per head at purchasing power parities is a part of that measure, but does not present a full picture in itself.

Income flows and wealth effects

Income flows

Imagine the economy as a simple model where there are just households and firms. The **households** own all the factors of production — land, labour, capital and enterprise — and the **firms** are the producing units. Money moves from households to firms when they buy goods and services; and money moves back to households as payment for the use of the factors of production in the form of rent, wages, interest and profit. In this very simple model, known as the **circular flow of income** (Figure 1), money circulates from households to firms and back again, and the more that households spend and the more that firms produce, the higher the levels of income. It does not matter which way you look at it, the income and output in an economy should always be the same, and they are measured by **gross domestic product (GDP)**.

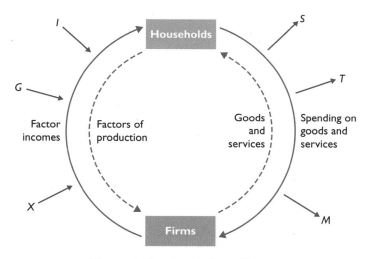

Figure 1 The circular flow of income

There are three **leakages** (or withdrawals) from the circular flow of income: savings, tax and imports. If you hide your money under your bed, the economy will slow down a little because there is less money in the circular flow. Similarly, if the government takes money away from the economy in the form of tax and does not spend it, or if people buy more things from abroad than they export, the economy will slow down as money leaves the circular flow. These three leakages effectively determine the size of the multiplier (see below).

By contrast, there are three **injections** into the circular flow. These are investment — which is an increase in the capital stock — government spending and exports. These all increase the circular flow and a change in any of these will be magnified by the multiplier.

Examiner tip

The multiplier is a factor that shows the change in total income as compared to an initial injection. So a multiplier of 2 means that a £1 billion injection will increase incomes by £2 billion (including the initial injection).

Knowledge check 18

Is consumption an injection into the circular flow?

Knowledge check 19

Is it true that an increase in house prices (wealth) will cause a fall in aggregate demand, because people don't have as much money to spend on other things?

Examiner tip

A wealth effect is the effect on incomes or spending when asset values change.

The **multiplier** is the number of times a change in incomes exceeds the change in net injections that caused it. It is the knock-on effect on incomes when injections and withdrawals change. For example, if there is a £10 million increase in export values, the inward flow of money to the UK will be re-spent within the UK. When the money is spent it will become other people's incomes. These incomes will be re-spent, and so on.

The importance of the multiplier is that if there is any change in spending in an economy, the final impact on incomes will be much greater than the initial impact. The greater the leakages, the smaller the multiplier. The formula is based on how much of any extra pound earned is re-spent within the economy: that is, **the marginal propensity to consume**. The size of the multiplier in the UK is approximately 1.4, but in developing countries it is often higher, which partly explains their higher growth rates. For example, in a country with a multiplier of 3, a net injection of $10 million will cause a $30 million increase in incomes in total.

If all the injections equal all the leakages, then the economy will be in **equilibrium**; if injections are greater than leakages, the economy will grow; and if leakages are greater than injections, the economy will contract.

Wealth effects

Wealth is the sum of all the assets in an economy. In the UK, much wealth is held in the form of housing (41%); the other major forms of wealth are stocks and shares and capital assets. Wealth is a **stock** concept, whereas income is a **flow** concept — this means that wealth does not have a direct impact on the circular flow of income, but changes in wealth are likely to have an effect on incomes and spending. For example, if you live in a property that increases in value, you might feel more confident about spending in the economy and your increased spending will then become part of the circular flow of income. Moreover, if houses become more expensive, someone could go to their mortgage provider and request mortgage equity release: that is, take out a loan based on the increased wealth. When that loan is spent, the circular flow increases. By contrast, when capital markets take a downturn in the USA, people living on pensions in the UK might find that their incomes fall because dividends on pension funds are often based on capital gains of shares.

Useful exercises

- The best site for mortgage information is **www.bbc.co.uk** — on the news page go to 'Business', then 'Economy', or watch a recent clip under 'Video and audio'. Then you might also visit **www.mortgagesmadeeasy.co.uk**, **www.cml.org.uk** (the website of the Council of Mortgage Lenders) or **www.mortgageguideuk.co.uk** for accessible explanations and arguments about anything to do with mortgages.

Summary

- Income (e.g. export income) is a flow concept, while wealth (e.g. capital assets) is a stock concept. Income is measured by real GDP. Wealth in the UK is £6.7 trillion — five times the total income in the economy. See **www.statistics.gov.uk** for the latest figures. Most wealth in the UK is held in the form of housing (41%). The rest is split fairly equally between capital assets and shares. Capital assets or stock in the UK amount to £3.1 trillion. This is slightly less than the cost of maintaining all capital stocks in their current condition — a cost known as depreciation.

- Changes in income have multiplier effects on the level of total spending in the economy. An increase in injections has a proportionately larger effect on GDP.

- Changes in leakages affect the size of the multiplier. The larger the leakages (S, T and M), the smaller the multiplier effect will be.

- Changes in asset values have a direct impact on incomes and spending. This is called the wealth effect.

Aggregate demand and supply

'Aggregate' means *added together* — the individual elements that were introduced in microeconomics are totalled in macroeconomics. Aggregate demand and supply analysis brings together the amount that consumers wish to consume and firms wish to produce at any price level. **Aggregate demand (AD)** is the total planned expenditure on goods and services produced in the UK. **Aggregate supply (AS)** is the total planned output of goods and services. The equilibrium point where they meet determines the average price level and the equilibrium real output level. The price level can be measured by a price index such as the CPI, and the output by real GDP.

The aggregate demand and supply model is probably the most useful tool for macroeconomists, because it gives reasons for changes in the important macroeconomic variables: when price levels increase this is inflation, and when output increases this is economic growth.

Aggregate demand

Aggregate demand (AD) is the total planned expenditure on goods and services produced in the UK. It comprises consumption (C), investment (I), government spending (G) and exports (X) minus imports (M).

The AD curve is downward sloping. This is not because 'people buy more things when they are cheaper' (the most common misunderstanding about the AD curve). There are three ways to explain the downward-sloping AD curve, any of which is adequate for an answer at AS:

- Lower prices in an economy mean increased international competitiveness, so there are more exports and fewer imports. In other words, net exports are higher at lower prices.
- The total amount of spending will be approximately equal whether prices are high or low because people have approximately the same amount of money to spend, so

the area under the curve will be fairly constant. This is known as the **real balance effect**. If you plot a constant area, you will get a **rectangular hyperbola**.

- At higher price levels, interest rates are likely to be raised by the monetary authorities. This means that investment, a component of aggregate demand, will fall and savings might increase.

The components of aggregate demand and their relative importance

Consumption

Consumption, or spending by households on goods and services, is the main component of aggregate demand, comprising approximately 65%. It measures the amount that consumers wish to spend at various price levels. One of the key determinants of consumption is the confidence of the consumer, both in terms of job security and in terms of future income prospects. If consumers are feeling confident, they are more likely to make large purchases which they can pay for in the future. Another determinant is interest rates. Higher interest rates not only leave consumers with less spending money after housing costs, but also increase the cost of hire purchase. A third determinant is the housing market. When house prices accelerate upwards, home owners can extract more equity from their houses, as discussed in the section on 'Wealth effects' (p. 20).

Investment

There is an inverse relationship between interest rates and the level of investment that firms intend to make. This is because increases in the capital stock have to be financed, and there is an opportunity cost to that finance. Firms often borrow from banks to finance investment, so if interest rates rise, the cost of borrowing rises and firms are less likely to borrow, and therefore less likely to invest. However, investment is not based solely on interest rates, and some argue that the interest elasticity of demand for investment is very low. This is because investors are sometimes driven more by other factors, such as confidence in future sales patterns, what their main competitors are doing, government incentives and regulations, and the prospects for future interest rates than by the current rate of interest.

A change in investment will change the level of aggregate demand, but a change in aggregate demand will also change the level of investment. This circular relationship can be analysed using the **accelerator**, and although this is not required knowledge for the AS examination, it is a useful way of evaluating the role of investment.

Government spending

Government spending in the UK comprises almost 40% of all spending in the economy, totalling about £590 billion. Government spending need not equal tax revenue and the difference between them is known as a **budget (or fiscal) deficit or surplus**. The government can deliberately manipulate aggregate demand by overspending (running a budget deficit) when there is a slowdown in the economy, and vice versa in a boom. Taxing more heavily in times of abundance is a useful way to put the brakes on the economy, although sometimes governments miscalculate the start of the downturn and cut taxes too early (many criticised George Osborne's measures for this, coming out of the recession in 2011). Similarly, net spending can be increased in a recession, which will reverse the effects of demand deficiency.

Another factor to consider is the **national debt** — the accumulation of budget deficits over the years. Governments hope that the budget will balance over the course of the next 5 years for current spending at least (not investment), otherwise the government will accrue national debt. Interest payments have to be made on this, and if the government continues to overspend there will be a cost for future generations. In the short run, however, there is some flexibility with the balance of the government's accounts.

Assessing the impact of an imbalance in the flow of government income

The Keynesian view is that fiscal policy — that is, the deliberate manipulation of government spending and taxation in order to change aggregate demand — is a powerful tool in shifting aggregate demand, made much more effective by the working of the multiplier. In contrast, the classical economists' view is that overspending by the government has a similar effect to printing more money — it is purely inflationary.

There is now some consensus that deliberate fiscal manipulation has a short-run impact on output, but only if wage demands and other cost pressures are kept in check. Until the credit crunch and recession hit the economy in general in 2008, there was much consensus that it is only really through supply-side policies that long-term improvements in equilibrium employment will be achieved, as the *AS* curve shifts to the right (see 'Shifts in the aggregate supply curve', pp. 26–27). With the prospect of a repeat of the economic depression that followed the 1929 crash, Keynesian expansionary budgets again became popular. As Keynes would say, 'in the long run we are all dead': that is, by the time the unemployed become employable, they will be past employment age, and sometimes the government must not sit by and let the economy go into a deep slump, but instead stimulate the circular flow through fiscal policy.

Net exports

Exports represent an injection into the circular flow of income, in that the money paid for goods and services sold abroad enters the domestic flow of income. Imports mean that there is an outflow of money, and exports minus imports gives the total movement of funds, known as **net exports**. (If the value of imports is greater than the value of exports, this will be a negative figure, as in the UK.) There are several reasons why the value of net exports might change.

First, consider a change in the exchange rate. If the exchange rate increases in value against other currencies, imports become cheaper and exports more expensive on world markets. Over time, people respond to these relative price movements and the demand for exports falls and the demand for imports rises. A stronger currency will worsen net exports, whereas a weaker currency will improve the figure.

However, in the short run the price elasticity of demand for exports and imports tends to be low. This may be because contracts have been signed for specific deals in international trade, or because the traded components are a very small percentage of firms' overall costs. For example, an Italian importer of BMW Minis will agree a price

in advance of delivery from the UK. If the pound gets stronger against the euro, the price of the cars will remain as per contract. Price elasticity of demand may also be low because of a lack of available substitutes, as in the case of oil. Owing to the low price elasticity of demand for exports and imports, the initial impact of a change in the exchange rate may be the opposite of the one described above.

A second major cause of changes in the value of net exports is changes in the global economy. For example, if there is a recession in the USA, but the UK does not suffer a slowdown, the USA will buy fewer exports from the UK, and will be attempting to export more. Similarly, if there is inflation in the UK, but not in other countries, net exports from the UK will worsen as UK goods become increasingly uncompetitive. A collapse in a stock market in another part of the world may also have direct effects on UK exports via wealth effects.

Thirdly, non-price factors, such as quality and after-sales service, are major determinants of net exports. Germany, for example, cannot compete effectively on price, but the value of its exports exceeds that of any other country owing to its high quality of design and manufacture.

In summary, when any of the components C, I, G or X rises, the AD curve shifts to the right (see Figure 2). The same happens if imports fall. As a useful evaluation point, it is wise to consider that the above analysis involves changes in *levels* rather than *rates*. In the UK these components do not usually fall, but they may rise more slowly during an economic slowdown, which means that the AD curve will still shift to the right, but by increasingly smaller amounts.

Examiner tip
When referring to aggregate demand, always bear in mind the components, C + I + G + (X − M), and try to find ways to refer to the **multiplier**.

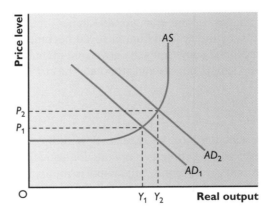

Figure 2 Effect of a shift in aggregate demand on price and real output

Aggregate supply

Aggregate supply is the amount that firms are willing to produce at various price levels. It is largely influenced by productivity, which in turn is influenced by factors such as the costs of production, the level of investment, the availability and efficiency of factors of production and supply-side policies.

There are two views of aggregate supply. The classical view is that in the long run an economy will operate at full capacity and there will be no unemployed resources in the economy: that is, the *AS* curve is vertical. If there are any unemployed resources, the prices of these factors will fall until the surplus disappears.

By contrast, the Keynesian view is that the equilibrium level of output can occur below the full employment level of output. According to this view, the *AS* curve has a backward-bending L shape, with three distinct sections: spare capacity, bottlenecks and full employment. The assumption behind this analysis is that an economy can be at equilibrium when it is not at full employment. In other words, demand deficiency may mean that unemployed resources such as labour will not find work if the economy is left to its own devices.

In section A of Figure 3 there is spare capacity. The economy can increase output without any cost pressures. This is because there are unused resources, such as factories not working at full capacity, or unemployed labour. In this section, aggregate demand might shift to the right — for example, through fiscal policy — and equilibrium real output would increase without causing an increase in the price level. The situation is comparable to that of Japan over the past two decades, where there is a lot of scope for increased production, but unemployment persists in the long run.

Examiner tip
For the AS course, you can draw the AS curve with straight lines and still earn all the available analysis marks. However, if you draw an AS curve with a sense of spare capacity or full capacity (that is, an upward-sloping curve), you will find it easier to pick up evaluation marks.

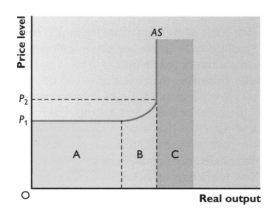

Figure 3 The Keynesian aggregate supply curve

Section B in Figure 3 is the bottlenecks section, where some constrictions in the supply chain cause cost and wage pressures to build up in some areas of the economy. This usually involves a certain type of labour which when in short supply can have its price bid upwards. An example concerns the shortage of construction workers associated with the HS2 High Speed road link between London and Birmingham. If aggregate demand expands in this section of the graph, then while the economy will still grow, there will be some inflation because in order to attract enough construction workers, the scheme operators will have to raise wages to draw workers away from other jobs.

Section C illustrates full capacity in the economy. All viable workers have work, so if a firm wants to take on more workers it will have to entice them away from other jobs by offering higher wages. In this section of the diagram, if aggregate demand increases, although in the short run there might be some extra spending, the long-term effect will be increased inflation and no increased output.

Knowledge check 22

Do all economists draw the AS curve as upward sloping?

According to the classical view, section C is the only part of the AS curve that occurs. The economy cannot be in equilibrium while there is unemployment. So, if unemployment does exist, it can only result from a short-run failure of the market or from mismanagement by the government.

Shifts in the aggregate supply curve

Shifts in aggregate supply occur when factors change which will affect most firms. Such factors might relate specifically to the cost of workers (labour market) or the way in which firms compete (product market). Let's consider how changes in both markets might produce a rightward shift of the AS curve.

Labour market

In the labour market, a rightward shift in the aggregate supply curve could occur in the following ways:

- **Productivity gap closes.** Productivity is output per unit of input, and if it increases relative to a country's main trading partners then the productivity gap is said to be closing. For example, the gap is currently closing between the UK and France, so while the UK has lower productivity than France, its productivity is increasing over time, which means that costs of production are becoming relatively less expensive in the UK compared to France. However, the gap is widening between the UK and the remainder of its major trading partners.
- **Education and skills improve.** Increased spending on education and training should mean that a country's workforce can produce more output per worker. Education increases the value of the potential output. However, not all education achieves this end. It is not clear that a BA in Madonna Studies or a BSc in Surf Science has a major impact on costs of production in the UK.
- **Health spending increases.** An increase in resources in the health sector should mean that workers have fewer days off sick and are active for longer — often beyond traditional retirement ages. However, spending on health might be absorbed into wage increases for staff in the health service, which would have little overall effect on the level of healthcare. Similarly, the majority of healthcare spending goes on the elderly or very young, neither of which is economically active.

Product market

Examiner tip

Make sure that you know three supply-side policies in good detail. Make sure they are not demand-side policies or trade policies. Remember that subsidies and privatisation might not be the best solutions to problems such as low levels of productivity in the current context for the UK.

In the product market, a rightward (or downward) shift in the aggregate supply curve could occur in the following ways:

- **Sources of raw materials change.** In a developed country like the UK most raw materials are imported, and if global competition increases, UK costs will fall. The cost of these imports depends on demand pressures from other parts of the world as well as supply. If there is a global increase in demand for oil, for example, this will cause the costs of production to increase in the UK because oil is a major production cost in almost all UK firms.
- **Exchange rates fall.** If the euro fell in value relative to the pound, many costs would fall in the UK, meaning that aggregate supply in the UK increases.
- **International trade increases.** As a country opens up to more trade, competition drives down prices and inefficient domestic firms give way to overseas firms with a comparative advantage. So as globalisation develops, aggregate supply increases.

- **Technological advances.** Innovation and investment in new ideas tend to reduce costs for all firms. For example, widespread access to the internet increases competition among firms and also means that firms can be more streamlined. Buying a book, for instance, is now much cheaper online because there are fewer expensive retail outlets to maintain.
- **Regulation changes.** There are many regulations in the UK economy which have been imposed to try to maintain a disciplined economy, for example in the postal and telecommunications services. However, such industries have been increasingly deregulated over the past two decades to increase competition, which in turn imposes its own form of discipline. The net effect is that parcel postage and phone services — costs faced by all firms — have reduced in real terms, shifting aggregate supply to the right (or down).

Common examination errors

- Many students get very confused when drawing *AD/AS* diagrams, either using microeconomic labels (*D* and *S*) or shifting *AD* and *AS* in the wrong directions. It is best to use simple versions of the diagrams that you understand.
- Many AD/AS diagrams are drawn in exams — and, indeed, in some textbooks — with inflation rather than the price level on the vertical axis. Use the price level label for simplicity.

Links and common themes

- The relationship between exchange rates and net exports can most clearly be understood using the Marshall–Lerner condition and the J curve. This will be explained in Unit 4.
- Fiscal policy is discussed further on p. 37 of this guide, and developed more fully in Unit 4.

Examiner tip

You will be required to draw *AD/AS* diagrams in your exam, so you might like to sketch all the possible permutations and put them on separate cards. Then rank them in order for the way in which you would use them to solve various macroeconomic problems.

Knowledge check

23–25

For each of the following, decide whether *AD* or *AS* changes, or both. Then decide whether they increase or decrease. Are these short-term or long-term changes?

23 a cut in education spending

24 a rise in interest rates

25 an increase in productivity relative to our main trading partners

---

- Aggregate demand is the total amount that is planned to be spent in an economy at any price level.
- Aggregate supply is the output that all firms are willing to supply at any price level.
- Equilibrium real output and price level occur where aggregate demand meets aggregate supply.
- The components of aggregate demand are $C + I + G + (X - M)$ and a change in any one of these will shift the *AD* curve, with multiplier effects.

- If aggregate demand increases, the price level is likely to rise and output may rise, depending on the price elasticity of the aggregate supply curve.
- Increases in aggregate supply will tend to lower prices or curb rises in prices. Real output is likely to increase, although this depends on the elasticities where the *AD* and *AS* curves cross.

Summary

Economic growth — causes, constraints and costs

Actual growth can be defined as an *increase in real GDP* and **potential growth** as an *increase in capacity* in the economy. Measures of real GDP tend to fluctuate over the course of an economic cycle. During a **boom**, real GDP rises fast. In a **recession**, it falls for at least two consecutive quarters. During a **slowdown**, the level of GDP may be rising, but rising below the trend, or GDP might be falling.

The difference between *actual output* and either the *trend* or *potential output* is called the **output gap**.

One way of drawing the output gap is shown in Figure 4.

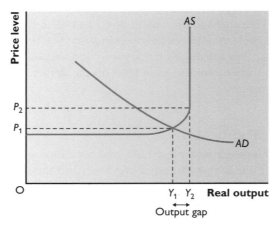

Figure 4 The output gap shown as the difference between actual output and potential output

If the economy is growing faster than the trend, pressures will grow in the economy, such as tight labour markets, wage pressures and shortages of raw materials. This is referred to as a **positive output gap**. It may be a sign that the economy is overheating and the inflationary pressures might persuade the Bank of England's Monetary Policy Committee to raise interest rates. However, if the economy is growing below trend, there is likely to be spare capacity in the economy. This situation is known as a **negative output gap**. It means that there is scope for a cut in interest rates, which is less likely to cause inflationary pressures.

Causes of *actual* economic growth

Economic growth can occur because there is an increase in one of the components in **aggregate demand**, where $AD = C + I + G + (X - M)$.

Here are some examples. Increased consumption might occur because of increased consumer confidence or the availability of credit. Increased investment increases the level of growth, and is itself dependent on the level of growth (i.e. it has an **accelerating** effect on growth rates). Government spending on education or health

Examiner tip
If there is an output gap, the country is not growing at the trend or the potential output.

Examiner tip
A negative output gap means that the country is not using its resources to the full. There could be an increase in output without opportunity cost in terms of inflation.

might cause growth. Export-led growth has the added advantage of improving the current account of the balance of payments.

Growth can also occur because of an increase in **aggregate supply**. This might happen because costs of production fall — for example, labour markets might become more competitive thanks to immigration or an increase in the birth rate — or because of government supply-side policy such as **deregulation** in the markets (removing constraints that limit competition). This is discussed in the section on 'Policy instruments', pp. 36–43.

A shift of the *AD* or *AS* curve to the right should cause an increase in actual growth. However, if aggregate demand increases and the *AD* curve is crossing the vertical part of the *AS* curve, the only effect will be increased prices, not increased GDP. Similarly, if aggregate supply increases and the *AD* curve is crossing the *AS* curve on its horizontal part, there will be no change in the equilibrium and there will be no change in price levels or output.

Causes of *potential* economic growth

Potential economic growth can occur only when the vertical part of the *AS* curve shifts to the right, increasing the amount that the economy could produce. Using another model, potential economic growth increases when the production possibility curve shifts to the right. Possible causes of the *AS* shift are described in the previous section as well as later in this guide in the section on 'Policy instruments', pp. 36–43.

Constraints on growth

There are several factors constraining growth:

- **Absence of capital markets.** One of the main reasons why Latin America grows more slowly than the Asian subcontinent is that Asia has more credible and efficient capital markets. In many economies in sub-Saharan Africa, the interest charged on credit, if credit is available at all, is typically over 50%. One of the issues is the **asymmetric information** in credit markets, where the lender knows very little about the borrower and charges higher rates to cover the enormous risk. The only people able to afford these high rates are likely to be among the more corrupt borrowers, which makes it even less likely that people will lend. The market then becomes a **missing market**, in the sense that there is no equilibrium price of credit where buyers and sellers can agree a rate of interest.
- **Government instability.** Where governments are incompetent, or lack transparency or strong political backing, the economy cannot attract inward investment and the currency might be unstable. The government might have a fiscal deficit which means that it has little power to spend money to encourage growth. This is more extreme if there is political tension, war or diversion of funds to increase a country's defence.
- **Labour market problems.** A shortage of skilled labour is a major constraint on growth. As countries get richer, birth rates tend to fall dramatically; in the long run this means that the labour supply will fall. One of the most effective policies for reducing this in high-income countries is to allow increased immigration, although in low-income countries the exit of skilled workers (known as the 'brain drain') exacerbates the skill problems.

Knowledge check 26
What is the difference between actual and potential economic growth?

Examiner tip
Economic growth is most useful to economists when presented without the effects of inflation — that is, as real or constant values. If you are given nominal or current values, you will gain marks by commenting that the figures are distorted by inflation.

- **External constraints.** Trade is a key driver of growth. Uneven access to world markets owing to tariffs and subsidies can prevent a country from growing. Global recession or fears of terrorism also slow down trade, as does volatility in exchange rate markets. Figures suggest that for every 3% growth in world trade there is a 1% increase in world GDP, and therefore anything that holds back international trade is likely to act as a constraint on growth.

Benefits of growth

Growth benefits employees, firms and governments in the following ways:

- **Employees.** Incomes and wealth rise when there is economic growth. Standards of living rise as long as the costs of living do not increase at the same rate. In other words, *real* growth means that *real* incomes rise. Increases in growth can mean that wealth in the form of assets such as shares and houses increases.
- **Firms.** Firms tend to make more profit when there is economic growth. In times of growth, consumer spending usually rises, which means that firms sell more. As revenues and profits rise, firms can take on more workers and are more likely to invest. This increases future growth prospects.
- **Governments.** When incomes and assets rise in price, people pay more income and capital gains tax. Governments also have fewer demands to pay unemployment benefits. So in times of economic growth the government is likely to enjoy a healthier fiscal position.

Costs of growth

Despite the benefits listed above, growth incurs the following costs:

- **Income inequality.** The unwaged and unskilled are less likely to benefit from increased incomes. While money might eventually 'trickle down' to lower-income groups, there might equally be a two-speed economy where the incomes of some people accelerate but others cannot get out of a low-skill slow lane. The type of production tends to change during periods of economic growth, so there is likely to be short-term unemployment for people who do not have labour market flexibility.
- **Environmental problems.** Depletion of natural resources and external costs such as carbon emissions and other forms of pollution are likely to increase with economic growth. However, high-income governments can use their increased tax revenue to clean up the environment.
- **Balance of payments problems on the current account.** With higher incomes, domestic consumers suck in more imports and there is less incentive for firms to export. However, if growth were export-led, the current account would improve.
- **Bottlenecks in the economy.** When there is little spare capacity in the economy, factors of production such as skilled labour and fuel rise in price. Monopoly power might also develop, which can be used as a barrier to the entry of new firms (see Unit 3). This can be shown using an increasingly inelastic AS curve.
- **Social dislocation and stress.** Higher incomes have to be earned. With increased pay there are usually increased responsibilities. There may be more travel and the need to move further afield as firms grow. However, with higher incomes people can also afford to work fewer hours, go on more luxurious holidays, pay for their children's education or retire early. So social life may or may not improve as the economy grows.

- **Problems of rapid growth.** Rapid growth can cause short-term spikes in prices. If a country grows too quickly there might be bad planning, corner cutting and shoddy workmanship. However, rapid growth might just need time to settle down in terms of income distribution, and a strong government such as that in China can ensure that growth is planned effectively.

Knowledge check 27

Is there any validity in saying 'If there is increased growth there will be inflation'?

Useful exercises

- Figures for the output gap in OECD countries are published by the OECD every year. In these figures, a positive output gap is a boom and a negative output gap is a slump. The UK and Germany had slumps in 2008–10. Name another country for which this is true.
- Read an account of London in the winter of 1947, when smog brought the capital to a standstill. To what extent can economic growth be used to explain problems of smog and the cleanliness of much of London in recent years?

Links and common themes

- Asymmetric information (in capital markets) has been introduced in Unit 1 and is useful for explaining limits to growth.
- To understand more about asymmetric information in the credit market, read George Akerlof's short article on lemons in 'An economic theorist's book of tales', obtainable cheaply on the internet.
- Constraints on growth in developing countries will be discussed fully when considering limits to growth and development in Unit 4.

- Economic growth can be explained in terms of increases in actual GDP or increases in potential GDP. When aggregate demand increases, actual GDP will increase, as long as the *AS* curve is not vertical. When aggregate supply increases, actual GDP will increase, as long as the *AD* curve does not cross the *AS* curve on a horizontal part of the curve. Only a shift of the *AS* curve to the right will cause an increase in potential economic growth.

- The benefits and costs of growth are not easy to measure, and they change over time. It is therefore difficult, but important, to assess whether the benefits outweigh the costs. As growth rates rise, it is likely that the increasing marginal costs will be outweighed by decreasing marginal costs.

Summary

Macroeconomic objectives of governments

There are six main objectives that governments generally wish to pursue:
- increased economic growth (rises in real GDP)
- control of inflation
- reduction in unemployment
- restoration of equilibrium in the balance of payments on current account

- a more equal distribution of income
- protection of the environment

The order of priority varies according to the politics of a particular government and institutional arrangements such as the Monetary Policy Committee. Some governments see the control of inflation as the most important macroeconomic goal. Others, such as governments with a socialist leaning, would focus on the redistribution of incomes and the reduction of unemployment.

Trends in macroeconomic measures

In the years before the last UK recession of 2008–10, the UK saw economic growth at a trend of between 2 and 3% per annum for 15 years, and inflation hardly reaching 3%, but in 2008 growth became negative in the wake of the credit crisis, and inflation was persistently above the ceiling of the inflation zone for several years after that.

Unemployment, as measured by the Labour Force Survey, rose markedly after the credit crunch as the recession sank in, from 1.6 million at the start of 2008 to around 2.5 million in 2011.

The trade in goods of the balance of payments recorded a £46 billion deficit, just over 5% of GDP, while the current account deficit as a whole was £46 billion (3% of GDP) at the height of the boom in 2007. The pound has fallen 25% against the euro since 2008, which is by far the most important trading currency for the UK, and this is likely to lessen the deficit. But remember that in the short run a fall in the value of a currency tends to worsen the current account, because the price elasticity of demand for imports and exports is almost zero.

The distribution of income described on the national statistics website (go to UK Snapshots on **www.statistics.gov.uk**, then type 'income distribution' in the search box) shows a widening during periods of economic growth, but other factors that help to explain this uneven distribution include accelerating wages at the top end of the scale, a fall in male participation in the workforce, meaning an increasing number of workless households, and changes in the tax and benefit system.

Perhaps the least achieved government objective is the protection of the environment. Clear and unambiguous indications are given in national statistics on carbon emissions. The Kyoto Protocol, ratified by 170 countries (but excluding the USA), states that by 2012 the developed countries will reach carbon emission levels 5% below their 1990 levels. Although the UK has seen some improvement, it fell far short of this target. The EU Emissions Trading Scheme system set up in 2005 has yet to lead to carbon reduction, but as the prices of permits rise this situation should improve.

While each of these objectives can have serious effects on economic agents if it is out of control, some clearly have a more immediate impact on people's lives. For instance, unemployment not only means lost income, but can mean a long-term reduction in a person's employability through loss of skills and training. However, it might be that the government cannot solve unemployment in the short term. Many economists believe that too much cushioning of the unemployed results in an inefficient labour market, and that competition and increased incentives for those out of work are a better approach to dealing with unemployment.

Examiner tip

The size of the current account deficit tends to be reduced in a recession. We buy fewer imports, and the incentive to export increases.

Knowledge check 28

State one reason why unemployment benefits should be increased, and one why they should be decreased.

Similarly, inflation of 2% is not thought to be a problem, and as long as incomes move in line with inflation there will be no serious side-effects. Most people's wages, and also student grants and pensions, are adjusted in line with inflation, and so reducing inflation below this level is not a priority. However, as inflation rises there comes a point where it erodes international competitiveness, discourages foreign inward investment, and causes income redistribution away from savers to borrowers to such a degree that its destabilising effects become a major concern.

A current account deficit on the balance of payments is of no concern to governments if there is enough trust in the capital markets and the value of the currency. It is, however, a sign that the country may be overspending relative to its income and at some point the outflow of money will have to be compensated by inflows. The UK has international investments abroad with enormous earning potential, which may mean that the balance will be restored if the situation is left to itself (**laissez faire**). Many economists therefore think that the UK government should not try to rectify a current account deficit with demand management. However, most agree that supply-side policies should be used to restore competitiveness in the long run.

Perhaps the most contentious of policy objectives is the idea of taxing the rich and giving to the poor. Social spending by the UK government on income support accounts for about a third of government expenditure — five times the amount spent on defence. Many would argue that redistributing income from the rich to the poor through taxes and benefits is simply unfair, destroys incentives and reduces the work ethic. The main drawback with social expenditure is that it has little effect on reducing poverty; some argue that it can even create a 'dependency culture'. While this might be true in general, extreme poverty is debilitating and leaves potential workers caught in a cycle of worklessness. They may be unable to sustain permanent employment at the available rates of pay due to personal circumstance, dependants, a lack of skills or the high cost of housing.

Useful exercises

- Look at the UK fact sheets available at **www.esrc.ac.uk** — this respected academic research institution is a valuable resource for the whole A-level course. Follow the 'Facts and figures' link — the 'UK fact sheets' are within this. There are pages on productivity and distribution of wealth, to name just two.
- To see a breakdown of government spending, go to **www.hm-treasury.gov.uk**, access the webpage for the latest budget, click on the 'Summary of key points' and look at the final page showing where taxpayers' money is spent. These objectives are revisited in more depth when considering the role of the state, in Unit 4.

Summary

- The priority given to the six macroeconomic objectives depends on the political stance of any particular government. The aim of government is often not to reach a zero rate of, say, unemployment or inflation, as this would cause increased pressures elsewhere in the economy. It usually seeks a balance between the objectives (see the section on 'Conflicts between objectives', pp. 34–36). The government does not itself finance a deficit on the balance of payments. A deficit could, however, cause a fall in the UK banking system's reserves of foreign currency and result in a downward movement in the value of the currency — it is only in this respect that the government aims to maintain a balance, if at all.

Conflicts between objectives

In this section a limited range of conflicts has been chosen, although for each objective there are issues with every other objective. Some objectives, such as growth and employment, have more in common than others, such as growth and the environment. The degree to which there is conflict is a useful way to approach your evaluation.

Inflation and unemployment

Consider this scenario. You are running a nightclub and the DJ is asking you for a wage increase. She may be good at the job, but you are not keen to pay more for the same service because it will eat into profits. What do you do? If there were a whole selection of unemployed DJs eager and willing to take up the post, you would probably look to employ a replacement, at the same or possibly at a lower rate than your current DJ. If, however, DJs are in short supply and the success of your club depends on having a good DJ whom you can rely on, you would be more likely to enter into discussion with your current DJ to keep her on board.

In other words, a shortage of labour in a specific field can cause wage pressures to build up. The net effect in the wider economy is that, as wages go up, people start spending more, the costs of production increase because labour is a major production cost, and inflation begins to rise. In other words, low unemployment or reduced spare capacity leads to higher inflation.

This basic analysis is the rationale for the **Phillips curve**, which was an observation of an apparent trade-off between unemployment and inflation (measured by the rate of change in wages) in the UK between 1861 and 1913 (see Figure 5).

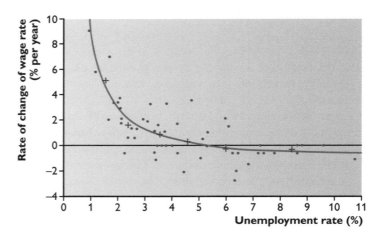

Source: 'The relationship between unemployment and the rate of change of money wages, 1861–1957', *Economica* (1958)

Figure 5 The relationship between inflation and unemployment in the UK, 1861–1913

In practice, if a government starts trying to exploit this trade-off it is unlikely to have the desired result. For example, because of the transparency of a government's

Examiner tip

The Phillips curve can be used to show that there is a trade-off between the objectives of low unemployment and low inflation.

actions, if it tries to spend its way into reducing unemployment, the most likely effect will be an increase in wages to absorb the government's extra spending: that is, inflation. As inflation goes up, newly employed workers will soon realise that their wages are being eroded by inflation, and firms will realise that they are not getting as much profit out of their workers because of inflation; therefore any increase in employment is not likely to last in the long term. For these reasons, while the Phillips curve is an observable phenomenon, it is not necessarily a viable tool for a government.

Economic growth and the balance of payments on the current account

As an economy grows and incomes rise, consumers are likely to demand more imports and firms' incentives to export will diminish, as it is easier to find eager customers in the domestic market. Therefore economic growth is likely to worsen the current account. The main exception to this is export-led growth, where the driver of growth is an increase in the export component of aggregate demand. Export-led growth means that the balance of payments will improve as more goods and services are sold abroad.

A second reason why growth might not necessarily worsen the balance of payments is if the growth is caused by an increase in aggregate supply. For example, owing to decreases in costs or increases in investment, an economy will become more internationally competitive, meaning that the economy can export more and import less while growing.

Increased employment and the sustainable environment

If more workers are being employed, there is likely to be more congestion on the roads and more carbon use because of more offices, more manufacture and greater energy usage. In addition, as people's incomes increase, workers are more likely to go abroad for their holidays, and most foreign travel will involve increased carbon emissions.

On the other hand, higher employment can mean that the government has more scope for taxation, and one spin-off might be the opportunity to use 'green' taxes, where taxation is specifically designed to reduce carbon use. For example, in the March 2008 budget the first year of road tax was doubled for new 'gas-guzzling' vehicles. The effect of higher employment also depends on whether the increase is in the manufacturing or service sector. As more people can work remotely in the service sector, it may be that an increase in employment has a negligible effect on the environment.

Economic growth and income redistribution

When an economy grows, incomes are most likely to rise at the top end of the income spectrum: for example, in the form of bonuses for sales executives. The effect is a widening of income inequality. However, over time, people at the high-income end of the scale may employ people from lower income groups, such as domestic staff. Increased demand for low-skilled labour should eventually lead to increased wages.

Knowledge check 29

If a government wants to cut unemployment, it might find that the level of wage inflation starts to rise, and this might cause inflation more widely. Why is this?

Nevertheless, many critics argue that, while there may be some transferred benefits of growth, there is a two-track labour market and those with low skills rarely benefit because, as skill shortages develop, immigration fills the gaps and the wages of low-skilled workers don't rise. Another counter-argument is that, even if wages rise by a constant percentage for everyone, income inequality will still increase in absolute terms.

Inflation and equilibrium on the balance of payments

Low inflation should help to improve a balance of payments deficit on current account. Low prices relative to other countries will mean that exports become more attractive on world markets and imports are less attractive. However, if the balance of payments tends to be in surplus, control of inflation will not restore equilibrium in the sense of removing a surplus.

Furthermore, when one of the main objectives of macroeconomic policy is to control inflation, interest rates might be tighter than they would otherwise be. High interest rates often mean that the exchange rate rises: 'hot money' flows in, as funds move between international capital markets seeking the best interest and exchange rates. A strong currency makes a country's exports less competitive and its imports relatively cheap, worsening the trade position in the long run as demand for exports and imports responds to the price changes.

Common examination errors

- While most students can draw and label a Phillips curve, few can explain why inflation would fall when unemployment rises, and vice versa. Even fewer can evaluate the concept.

Links and common themes

- There is a link with the externalities analysis in Unit 1, and the role of the state in Unit 4.

Knowledge check 30

Why does relatively low inflation improve the balance of payments on current account?

Knowledge check 31

Consider the effects of economic growth on the environment. Make a list of points to show why they conflict and then evaluate each point.

Knowledge check 32

Can you sketch a Phillips curve?

Summary

- The Phillips curve is an empirical observation that there is a negative correlation between inflation (via money wages) and unemployment.
- The Phillips curve is used by some to argue that there is a trade-off between unemployment and

inflation, and that if an economy can tolerate increased inflation then there would be lower long-term unemployment.

- Trade-offs can also be seen to exist between the other government macroeconomic objectives.

Policy instruments

Demand-side policies

Demand-side policy is a deliberate manipulation by the government of aggregate demand in order to achieve macroeconomic objectives. There are two demand-side policies: **fiscal policy**, which is the government's management of its spending and taxation with the aim of changing the total level of spending in the economy; and **monetary policy**, which is decision making using monetary instruments such as the interest rate.

Fiscal policy

If government spending is greater than taxation, the government is operating a **fiscal** or **budget deficit**. The net effect is to pump spending power into the economy. The **multiplier** magnifies the effect of this boost. So, for example, if the government builds a new hospital and does not pay for it all through current taxation, but instead borrows to finance the scheme, there will effectively be more spending power in the economy at the expense of spending power in the future. When the government pays for the workers and building materials for this hospital, the incomes will be re-spent in the economy, creating new incomes — which is the multiplier in operation. If an economy is going through a slowdown or a recession, then according to Keynesian thinking, the government should spend its way out of the recession.

By contrast, if government spending is less than taxation, there is said to be a **fiscal** or **budget surplus**, which takes spending power out of the economy with negative multiplier effects. The consensus among economists is that in times of boom or fast growth in the economy, the government should rein in its spending to curb inflationary pressures. This is known as **contractionary fiscal policy**, and it puts the government's accounts in a better position.

Does fiscal policy work?

In the UK, fiscal policy can only be implemented in the annual budget, although there is some room for manoeuvre in the autumn pre-budget report. This creates a time lag in decision making for fiscal policy, added to which there is an implementation lag because many tax changes cannot begin until the start of the new fiscal year in April, sometimes 1 or 2 years ahead. This means that if the government tries to respond to current economic problems using fiscal policy, the effect will not become apparent until the economy has started to change tack in the normal course of the economic cycle. Furthermore, when a government deliberately sets out to expand its spending, people will try to cash in on this by increasing their pay demands, and the effect will be increased wages and costs, rather than expanded output.

Next, there are **crowding-out effects** of increased spending by governments. For example, if the government decides to build a new hospital, there is less scope for a private hospital in the vicinity providing essentially the same service. There is also crowding out in the sense that when the government runs a deficit it needs to raise finance which, in times when credit is less readily available, will stifle private initiative. However, it can be argued that expansionary fiscal policy simply causes inflation because the debt issued to finance the expansion, often Treasury bills, is so liquid that it acts like printing money. There are many other critiques of fiscal policy and these are explored in Unit 4.

Monetary policy

The manipulation of monetary variables such as the interest rate has enormous implications across the whole economy. In the UK a group of up to nine economists forming the Bank of England's Monetary Policy Committee, whose sole purpose is the control of inflation, makes the interest rate decision independently of government. They meet at least once a month for a day and a half to examine evidence from across the country relating to inflationary pressures. They have a target for CPI inflation set for them by the chancellor of the exchequer, currently at 2% ±1%. If inflation falls outside the range of 1–3%, the governor of the Bank of England must write an open letter to the chancellor to explain why this has happened. In its first 10 years of operation, this occurred only once when inflation reached 3.1% in March 2007, but has risen significantly above 3% since May 2008 and by 2011 he had written ten letters (he has to write only one every three months if inflation remains above the ceiling).

Causes of inflation

In order to understand how monetary policy works it is important to consider the causes of inflation. In terms of *AD/AS* analysis, inflation can be shown as a shift to the right in *AD* or a shift to the left in *AS*. A shift to the right in *AD* is often called **demand-pull inflation** and it occurs whenever *AD* shifts to the right, usually exacerbated by multiplier effects. A shift to the left in *AS* is known as **cost-push inflation** and occurs whenever costs of production increase in an economy. These might be for short-term reasons, such as a fall in the exchange rate making imports more expensive, or for longer-term reasons such as higher corporation taxes.

However, according to monetarists such as Milton Friedman, inflation is 'always and everywhere a monetary phenomenon' (*Monetary History of the United States 1867–1960*, 1963). That is, monetarists believe that inflation is caused by increases in the money supply above the rate of the increase in the real output in the economy. Inflation can be controlled by controlling the money supply, either directly or more effectively perhaps through the rate of interest.

> **Knowledge check 33**
>
> What causes inflation?

Costs and benefits of inflation

Monetary policy involves controlling inflation, whether too high or too low. To judge whether the policy is worth pursuing, it is helpful to consider the costs of inflation and possible benefits of a little inflation.

The costs of inflation include:
- **Loss of international competitiveness.** Exports become relatively expensive and imports relatively cheap. The balance of payments is likely to worsen.
- **Redistribution of income.** Those on fixed incomes will find incomes fall in real terms. Those with index-linked incomes will not lose out, unless linked to a fairly unrepresentative measure such as the CPI.
- **Increased uncertainty.** If firms think that costs are rising and fear increases in interest rates, they might curb investment.
- **Investment from abroad might decrease.** Inflation erodes the value of money, so why buy into a currency that is falling in value?

Benefits of inflation might include:

- **Inflation reduces the real interest rate**, so cost of borrowing falls. Also, those with large debts such as mortgages find the real value of the debt will fall.
- Increased prices might be a sign that **firms can make more profits**. So in contrast to the above point about uncertainty, it might mean that investment is encouraged
- A little inflation provides a cushion against the perils of **deflation**. When prices are falling the economy can run into a vicious circle of underinvestment and spending.
- A little inflation means that **real wage differentials can be changed** without actually cutting money wages. The argument is that people will accept wage rises below the rate of inflation but will never accept wage cuts.

How monetary policy works

When interest rates are raised, the cost of borrowing rises. Consumers who borrow in order to finance their spending might be deterred from doing so and savers will be less keen to spend their savings because there is a greater opportunity cost in so doing. People with mortgages — of whom there are almost 10 million in the UK — will find their mortgage interest repayments rise, and will therefore be discouraged from spending, although those with fixed-rate mortgages will not suffer this immediately. Hire purchase — the method of buying major durable items, such as cars and white goods, on credit — will incur increasingly expensive monthly repayment instalments, which means that consumers might delay further major expenditures. House prices may fall as mortgages become less affordable, and this can cause negative wealth effects, where lower asset prices mean that people feel less inclined to spend and less able to take out loans based on the equity in their homes. Firms will find that investment is less attractive in many cases, and that fewer investments will make a return higher than the increased cost of borrowing. Therefore, firms will be less inclined to invest, which not only reduces current aggregate demand, but also has implications for long-term output prospects. The cost of exports might increase because interest rates are essentially a cost of production, so exports will fall and imports will rise. This is made even more likely when we factor in a very probable increase in the exchange rate, which occurs when 'hot' money is attracted to higher interest rates in the UK.

All these changes shift the *AD* curve to the left with multiplier effects. Depending on the shape of the *AS* curve, this may decrease both the price level and real output. Increasing interest rates can be an effective way of controlling inflation, but the cost is that economic growth also falls.

How effective is monetary policy?

Monetary policy has a shorter time lag than fiscal policy, although the Monetary Policy Committee estimates that interest rate changes can take 18 months to 2 years to have their full impact. There are further time delays because many mortgage holders have fixed-rate policies, which may delay the impact on their spending for some years. Furthermore, monetary policy is a very blunt tool that hits the whole economy, affecting both small and large firms, and rises in interest rates usually worsen income distribution. But perhaps the most significant criticism of monetary policy is that it raises costs of production in a situation where the cause of inflation

Knowledge check 34

What is the ideal rate of inflation for an economy?

Examiner tip
For your exam you will need to know that monetary policy involves manipulation of interest rates to achieve economic objectives. However, monetary policy can also involve quantitative easing, and you can earn valuable marks if you can discuss the use of increasing liquidity as a way of easing credit.

Knowledge check 35

If interest rate changes are not working, what else can be done to achieve economic objectives?

may itself be an increase in costs. So the rise in interest rates, rather than curing the problem, exacerbates it. In a time of rising commodity prices, the people who have to bear the brunt of this are those who have debts.

Supply-side policies

Supply-side policies include any action by the government intended to increase the amount that firms are willing to supply at any given price level. They involve improving the supply side of the economy: that is, productivity, availability of resources, tax or benefit incentives, removing regulations that add to costs or other cost reductions. In other words, they seek to shift the aggregate supply curve to the right (see Figure 6).

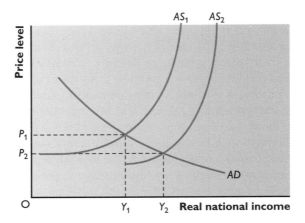

Figure 6 Effect of an increase in aggregate supply

There are three basics ways of achieving this:

- **Increasing price flexibility and signalling in a market.** If prices are not used to allocate resources effectively, there will be surpluses or deficits in the market. Suppose the government failed to increase the real rate of the minimum wage: this means that real wages would fall and there would be less unemployment in the labour market. Firms' real costs of production would therefore go down, and the *AS* curve would shift to the right.
- **Increasing competition.** Reducing artificial constraints such as legal monopoly rights, as in the UK Post Office, can increase competition. As firms compete, they must either cut costs or become more innovative in order to survive, which effectively shifts the *AS* curve to the right by reducing costs. Another way to increase competition is to privatise, although there is little scope left for privatisation of publicly owned firms in the UK. Deregulation is another option — this happened in the 1980s in the UK with the freeing up of the bus and coach operations sector.
- **Improving incentives.** Incentives function by giving people higher rewards for what they do, and therefore motivating them to work harder. The most obvious way to do this is to cut marginal tax rates. Longer-term solutions involve improving health, education and training, introducing performance-related pay and reducing corporation tax, which is a tax on a firm's profits. Again, these will encourage firms to produce more at any given price level.

Knowledge check 36

Are cuts in interest rates supply-side policies?

How effective are supply-side policies?

While some supply-side policies are clearly very effective — for example, deregulation in the phone industry has resulted in greatly improved standards in terms of price levels, after-care service and the like — there are some industries in which there is either no opportunity for increased competition, or where the benefits are outweighed by increased costs. For example, many believe that increased competition in the NHS has merely resulted in increased management costs rather than improved efficiency.

Another issue with supply-side policies is again the time lag. Some policies, most notably in education, can take many years to have any effect on production costs. If anything, in the short run they increase costs because there are fewer people in the labour market.

In addition, supply-side policies have side-effects on the demand side. For example, cutting taxes will have fiscal policy implications. Perhaps the most important aspect is that cutting minimum real wages and reducing trade union power affects lower-income earners adversely and disproportionately. However, effective supply-side policies do have the benign outcome of both lower inflation and higher rates of economic growth.

Examiner tip

Supply-side policies have a benign effect, in that they increase output at the same time as reducing pressure on prices, but there are also some costs.

Common examination errors

- The Monetary Policy Committee has a single target: inflation. It is incorrect to say that it aims to reduce unemployment or indeed has any other macroeconomic policy objective, although if inflation is under control, it might allow other areas of the economy to benefit from lower interest rates.

Useful exercises

- Read the minutes of the latest Monetary Policy Committee meeting at **www.bankofengland.co.uk**. List eight factors it has taken into account in making its interest rate decision, showing in each case how these relate to the price level in the UK.

Knowledge check 37

What will be the result of successful supply-side policies if there is a significant amount of spare capacity in the economy?

Links and common themes

- In taking this subject further in Unit 4, you will gain a more international perspective on these issues.

Summary

- Demand-side policies are used to shift the AD curve. They include fiscal and monetary policies.
- Supply-side policies are used to increase the aggregate supply in an economy. They involve measures which are often microeconomic in effect, in that they aim to influence individuals and firms to become more productive, cutting costs, improving incentives and increasing competitiveness, thereby being able to produce more at lower prices.
- Most governments use a combination of both types of policy to stabilise prices and maintain growth rates in the economy.

Knowledge check 38

What are macroeconomic policies?

Do macroeconomic policies conflict?

Fiscal policy and supply-side policy

Increased government spending may be used as part of a fiscal policy to increase aggregate demand, and much of this spending will be directed to the health and education sectors. In this case, fiscal and supply-side policies are working in tandem to improve growth prospects, and the supply-side effects may cancel out any ill effects on the price level from the expansion in demand.

Knowledge check 39

What is contractionary fiscal policy?

By contrast, if a government is using contractionary fiscal policy as a means of trying to control the price level, the impact might be a leftward shift of the *AS* curve, and therefore prices might rise rather than fall and output might contract even further than intended.

Fiscal and monetary policy

Examiner tip

Fiscal stance means the position that the government takes on fiscal policy.

While these are both demand-side policies, if a government runs a budget deficit, this has to be financed, which will affect the money markets. Much of the budget deficit is financed by issuing government 3-month Treasury bills, which offer investors secure and liquid assets that are easy to trade on the money markets. This helps with stability during a credit crunch, but at other times it might be inflationary because it increases liquidity available. A looser fiscal policy can mean that the Monetary Policy Committee favours a tighter monetary policy, taking into account the fiscal stance in deciding whether to raise interest rates.

Monetary policy and supply-side policy

A tight monetary policy means that interest rates are higher than they perhaps need to be. While this may control inflation, it increases costs for firms if they are borrowing money. By contrast, raising interest rates tends to make exchange rates rise. As UK firms import nearly all their raw materials, the effect on production costs may be significant. Therefore tight monetary policy can instead improve the supply side, although higher exchange rates are not guaranteed and they do harm firms trying to export. In the case of cutting interest rates, as in loose monetary policy, this can reduce borrowing costs for domestic firms, but if the exchange rate falls, firms will face increased import costs but gain competitiveness internationally.

Common examination errors
- Many answers mistake the impact of a change in the interest rate on the exchange rate. Usually they move in the same direction.

Useful exercises
- Look in the *Financial Times* for the prices of Treasury bills. Note that they do not earn interest — instead they are issued at a discount on their redemption price. Choose a bond and work out what the interest is: work out the discount on the time left before it is redeemed, then make this into an annual figure.

- Visit the website of the Institute for Fiscal Studies (**www.ifs.org.uk**) or the National Institute of Economic and Social Research (**www.niesr.ac.uk**), where you can get access to a simulation model of the whole economy on the web. You can then be your own chancellor, put in extra public spending, track the change in national income over time and see the multiplier at work.

Links and common themes

- You do not need an in-depth understanding of money markets, but there are links with the way shares work (Unit 1) and with the significance of public sector borrowing (Unit 4). If the government borrows heavily to finance a fiscal deficit, this increases the demand for short-term funds, and an increase in demand increases price, which in this case is the cost of borrowing: that is, the interest rate.

Knowledge check 40

If the government wants to borrow heavily, how does this affect the distribution of income?

Summary

- There are three macroeconomic policies that you need to know at AS. On the demand side there are fiscal and monetary policies, and on the supply side, supply-side policies. There are other macroeconomic policies, but you do not need to know them for Unit 2.

- Some analysts doubt that expansionary fiscal policy has any positive effects at all.

- Monetary policy is clearly powerful in controlling aggregate demand, but it is a blunt tool and has damaging effects on income distribution and across the supply side of the economy.

- Supply-side policies are now rather limited in their potential in the UK, and can cost a great deal for the government in terms of fiscal policy. However, policies aimed at increasing investment in the economy can have benefits in the future despite fiscal implications in the short run.

- A fiscal deficit means that the government needs to borrow from the money markets. This can produce two very different side-effects, depending on the type of credit available in the money markets. If there is a shortage of long-term funds, there may be crowding out as the government can offer good terms and security. But if money is lacking liquidity and the government borrows short term, issuing Treasury bills is a little like printing more money. This effectively loosens the money markets, which can be inflationary.

Questions & Answers

This section contains four data-response questions with student responses and examiner's comments that are designed to help you improve your understanding and examination technique. By seeing common examination errors in practice you can learn to avoid the common pitfalls. The student answers are graded A to C, with examiner's comments preceded by the icon to indicate where all the extra marks could be found.

Examination format

Unit 2 makes up 50% of the total marks in the AS examination (25% of the A-level). It is worth a maximum of 100 UMS marks. (UMS stands for the 'uniform mark system', which scales your actual mark to one that by statistical correction makes it equivalent to any other exam.) You will need to answer one question from a choice of two data-response questions, including a final mini-essay worth 30 marks, with total marks adding up to 80.

As a rough guide to the standard required, for the June 2010 examinations the A-grade boundary was set at an equivalent of 62/80, grade C at 46/80 and grade E at 32/80. A raw score of 78/80 scored full marks on the uniform system. However, you should be aware that these grade thresholds change according to the examiners' perception of the quality of the students and the difficulty of the papers. In other words, these boundaries are not uniformly applicable from one year to the next.

The amount of time allowed for the examination is 1 hour and 30 minutes. It is therefore advised that you spend 10 minutes reading through each part of the questions and sketching out a plan for each section. In this way you will have approximately the same time in minutes per question as there are marks allocated, although you would do well to go quickly on the 4- and 8-mark questions to allow yourself time to check through your whole paper at the end.

Assessment objectives

There are four assessment objectives, or sets of skills, in each unit of AS and A-level economics. When questions are set, these skills are very much in the mind of the examiners. The objectives are **knowledge**, **application**, **analysis** and **evaluation**. These are defined in the following table.

Objective	Assessment objectives
1 Knowledge and understanding	Identify the relevant economic points as outlined in the specified content.
2 Application	Use the data provided and other real-world data to apply economic knowledge and critical understanding to problems and issues.
3 Analysis	Break down economic problems and issues, using economic methodology.
4 Evaluation	Weigh up economic arguments and evidence, making informed judgements and justified conclusions.

In the overall assessment of the A-level, the four assessment objectives count equally. However, greater weighting is given to the first two objectives in AS, and to the final two objectives in A2. In the marking in the examples below, the first three objectives are referred to as 'KAA' and the fourth objective as 'Evaluation', and your examiners will use these abbreviations when they mark your papers.

Knowledge and understanding

This objective involves the ability to define key terms and to demonstrate an understanding of economic models relevant to the unit in question. In Unit 2 you are expected to be able to define terms such as inflation, productivity, supply-side policies and purchasing power parities (PPPs).

Application

The objective here is to show that you can apply macroeconomic theory to real-world data presented in the data-response questions. Anecdotal evidence may be used, such as a reference to events that you have read about recently. The latest movements in the main Bank of England interest rate might be relevant, for example, or the strength of the pound against other major currencies. The examination is a data-response paper rather than an essay paper, so you will need to refer to the data in order to earn full marks in this skill area.

Analysis

This assessment objective requires some economic theory to be used, in a logical way, to break down an argument. Often the best way of answering such questions is to use transmission mechanisms, which are logical economic stepping stones in your argument. For example, rather than just saying that a fall in interest rates might raise the level of aggregate demand, you could add a step saying that a fall in interest rates encourages people to take out more loans, and therefore consumer spending increases, which is likely to increase aggregate demand. If you then go on to describe the multiplier effect, you will receive high analysis marks.

Evaluation

The key here is to demonstrate critical distance from the issues being discussed. The mini-essay and two other sections of each question will require some evaluation, and this is indicated by command words such as 'to what extent', 'examine', 'discuss' and 'assess'. Of the 80 marks available for Unit 2, 20 are allocated to this skill, 12 of which are reserved for the mini-essay. Use signposts to mark out the evaluation element to help examiners to distinguish clearly between your script and those of others, with words such as 'however' and 'it depends'.

Methods for gaining evaluation marks include contrasting *short-term* with *long-run* effects, discussing the *for* and the *against* of an argument, criticising any *bias* presented in the data, drawing out the *wider context* of the discussion, and coming to a *reasoned conclusion*.

Grade boundaries

Performance descriptions have been set for the A/B and E/U boundaries by all A-level examining boards. These are split up into the four assessment objectives. The official Edexcel descriptions are reproduced below, with the author's own examples and comments in *italics*.

Knowledge

Grade A/B boundary	Grade E/U boundary
Candidates demonstrate detailed knowledge and understanding of a wide range of content, including terminology, institutions and models.	Candidates can demonstrate some knowledge from the specification, including terminology, institutions and models.

You do not need to know everything to get an A grade, but you should be able to make precise definitions of key terms such as the wealth effect.

Application

Grade A/B boundary	Grade E/U boundary
Candidates can apply the relevant toolkit (body of concepts, models, numerical and graphical techniques, theory and terminology) with clarity and incisiveness in familiar and unfamiliar scenarios.	Candidates apply some elements of the relevant economics toolkit in a range of scenarios.

You must be able to use *the data, and this is a skill that comes with practice. You should remember that the questions are drawn from the data, and it is your job to make that connection clear.*

Analysis

Grade A/B boundary	Grade E/U boundary
Candidates demonstrate, for the most part, ability to explain logically complex economic problems, models, theories and techniques.	Candidates demonstrate some ability to explain complex economic problems, models, theories and techniques, or more familiarity with economics problems and issues that are less complex.

This skill involves being able to break down an argument in a logical way. For example, working through the primary product market diagram is a basic skill, but understanding the declining terms of trade argument is more complex.

Evaluation

Grade A/B boundary	Grade E/U boundary
Candidates evaluate effectively straightforward economic arguments and evidence, for example by: prioritisation; making reasoned judgements; presenting well-supported conclusions.	Candidates demonstrate some ability to evaluate straightforward economic arguments and evidence.

Examiners in general enjoy marking scripts that are 'clear cut' rather than 'middle of the road'. The easiest way to place your script above the rest is to evaluate. Evaluation is not just about having an opinion or making an unsupported judgement. It is about justifying your arguments, developing your reasoning, seeing the value of alternative viewpoints and prioritising the options you have presented.

Even if you get parts of your answer wrong, you can still gain an A grade. Examiners apply *positive marking*, which means that what is of value will be accepted, but what is wrong will be ignored. Students often cross out a perfectly good piece of analysis. Leave the crossing out to the examiner — you might just earn some marks even if it isn't the best you can say.

In the examination, you will have 90 minutes and you will have to choose one from a choice of two questions. You should spend 10 minutes reading and choosing the question, giving you one minute per mark to earn a total of 80 marks. There is nothing worse than getting halfway through a question and realising that you would have been able to respond better to the other question.

Some questions are marked with an asterisk (*). This indicates that the quality of written communication will be taken into account by the examiner. The way that this is done is to award the balance of any doubt to the student in cases where an answer is expressed with clarity, but not in cases where there is obscurity in the response.

Question 1 **Indicators of economic performance**

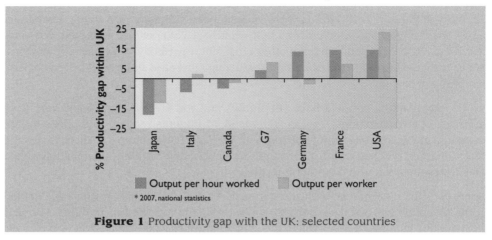

Figure 1 Productivity gap with the UK: selected countries

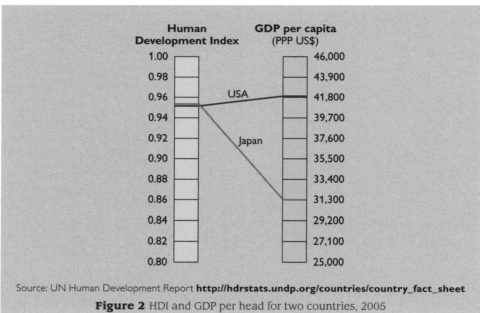

Figure 2 HDI and GDP per head for two countries, 2005

Table 1 Selected measures of economic performance, 2007 values

	GDP per capita (purchasing power parities, US$)	Life expectancy (years)	Human Development Index
USA	41,890	77.9	0.951
Japan	31,267	82.3	0.953
Republic of Korea	22,029	77.9	0.921
China	6,757	72.5	0.777

Source: United Nations Human Development Report, 2007/08

(a) Refer to Figure 1.

    (i) Explain what is meant by the term *productivity gap*. (4 marks)

ⓔ Productivity is a measure of how efficiently resources are used — that is, output relative to input. Don't confuse it with production.

    (ii) The UK is a G7 country. Using the data, explain how the G7 countries' productivity varies from the UK figure. (4 marks)

ⓔ This is a question about the UK being a base or comparator. The UK represents the base line in this data, or zero, so the other countries in the G7 must be more productive than the UK.

    (iii) Using an appropriate diagram, explain the likely effect of the change in productivity on the level of aggregate supply and the price level in a country such as Japan. (10 marks)

ⓔ In Unit 2 the diagram will almost certainly be an *AD/AS* diagram and a shift to the right would be an improvement in productivity. Don't forget to mark on the changes in equilibrium points and use a large arrow to show the shift.

(b) Using the data in Figure 2:

    (i) Outline one advantage and one disadvantage of using HDI figures to measure standards of living. (8 marks)

ⓔ Only one argument is needed on both sides of the issue, but students tend to list all the points that they have learned. Stick to an argument and develop it using data and analysis.

    (ii) *Assess two possible reasons why Japan and the USA have similar rankings for the Human Development Index, but are widely different for GDP at purchasing power parity. (12 marks)

ⓔ Although Japan has a much lower income per head, in terms of life expectancy and education its living standards are very similar to those in the USA. You can see that it is the health and education element that is making the difference, not the income.

    Remember the asterisk – you will be assessed on the quality of written communication. Use paragraphs, and keep your sentences short to make the meaning clear.

    (iii) HDI is a measure of economic development. Apart from HDI, examine the relative merits of two measures of economic development. (12 marks)

ⓔ Notice that this question is about development, not just growth, which means that you must take into account the quality of life rather than simply income per head. Here you are not restricted to the requirements of the HDI, so you can talk about any of the measures of development that you have studied: for example, access to clean water.

*(c) Seven out of the world's ten most polluting cities are in China. Assess the benefits and costs of growth for a country such as China, using the information provided in Figures 1 and 2 and Table 1.

(30 marks)

e Although it looks daunting, the 30 marks for the essay can be broken down into clearly defined sections which can be used for all the essays you will encounter in Unit 2. The formula is as follows: 2 marks for definition; 4 marks for diagram or further explanation of the key points or data use; 12 marks for three factors reasonably explained (3 × 4 marks), or two very well explained (2 × 6 marks); the final 12 marks for evaluation, again broken down as 3 × 4 marks for three reasonable points, or 2 × 6 marks for two well-developed points, or some combination of the two.

For this essay, choose at least one benefit and cost. Do not write out a full list of costs and benefits, but develop your points as fully as you can, using the data provided.

Student answer

(a) (i) The difference in output per unit of input between various countries. **a** It includes manufacturing and construction. It ignores productivity in areas such as farming (primary) and services (tertiary). **b**

e **4/4 marks awarded. a** Definition questions must always be brief but precise. Productivity must be distinguished from 'production' by looking at factor inputs as well as output, so use of the phrase 'per unit of input' makes this a good answer. **b** Data reference would be advised in any question which refers you to a source. Choose a country and quote the figures relative to the UK, e.g. Japan has 18% lower productivity than the UK.

(ii) The UK is represented by the zero line. This is used to make comparisons, usually in percentage change relative to the UK, so while the UK might be seeing productivity rise, the other G7 countries are seeing productivity rising even more. **a**

e **2/4 marks awarded. a** This shows adequate understanding of the concept, but there has been no reference to the data. The next step might have been to say that the non-UK G7 countries are around 5% more productive in terms of output per worker.

(iii) Increased productivity lowers the costs of production for firms because they can produce more output for the same factor costs. Aggregate supply increases, and price levels should fall. **a** This is because China has seen enormous rises in productivity. **b**

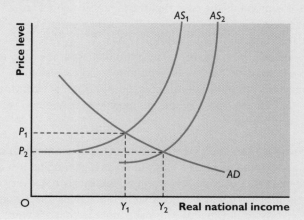

c

ⓔ 10/10 marks awarded. a The shift is described correctly, and the word 'costs' is used, which is crucial for AS questions (4 marks). **b** There is an attempt to apply the concept to China, and to use the evidence provided in Figure 1 (2 marks). **c** Four marks are earned for a fully labelled diagram. It shows the new and old price level — a detail that the examiner will be looking for. In cases such as this where the question is fully addressed, full marks will be given despite the brevity of the response.

(b) (i) Advantage: HDI stands for the Human Development Index. **a** The advantage of HDI is that it does combine the effects of increased growth with other quality of life indicators, and in that respect is an important measure of development. It might be worth comparing the HDI with other measures, some of which contain a GDP element and some that don't. **b**

Disadvantage: This index does not take account of poverty or other measures of deprivation, and in that respect is regarded by some as being of limited value.

ⓔ 4/8 marks awarded. The content of this answer is accurate but a little wordy. **a** There are no marks available for stating what HDI stands for, and there is opportunity cost in so doing. **b** It would be better to say more about the advantages and disadvantages as requested. For example, the HDI is a better measure of living standards than income alone, in that it takes into account health and education as well as the use of PPP values per head in real terms. School enrolment and life expectancy are among the most reliable indicators, providing data that are fairly easy to access and comparable across different countries. 2 marks awarded for identification only.

The main disadvantage could refer to 'income distribution', or a sense of the quality of education or the extra years lived. Political oppression or loss of a homeland is not measured, for example. 2 marks awarded for identification only.

(ii) Table 1 gives one main reason. The Japanese have a lower income per head but the life expectancy at 82.3 years is almost 5 years longer than the people in the USA.

The other possible reason is school enrolment. Although it is not shown in the table, it is probably the case that the Japanese school enrolment is higher than in the USA.

🅔 **8/12 marks awarded.** This is a good answer in that both reasons employ sound economics, and there is reference to the data. The only thing the answer lacks is evaluation. The answer could weigh up which is more likely: whether the data could be inaccurate, or whether things could change over time — for example, Japan's income per head might be about to fall, and in fact it has fallen since the data were produced.

(iii) One measure is GDP. This is the measure of total incomes in a country. If incomes go up then people are likely to enjoy higher standards of living which is a part of economic development. But this is not a very useful measure unless it is given 'per head' or in real values (taking out the effects of inflation). Also it doesn't take into account the cost of living.

🅔 **3/6 marks awarded.** GDP is arguably not a measure of economic development, although changes in real GDP per head might mean a change in development. So this is an unwise choice, although some credit is given for the evaluation.

Another measure is number of mobile phones per thousand of the population. With a mobile phone a farmer can get produce or a fisherman can get the catch to the market with the best price. Mobile phones act as a banking tool (for example, credit on phones can be used for trade) and can solve problems of poor credit in developing countries. Access to a mobile phone for a community can mean that health services can be accessed in an emergency. Mobiles transform the lives of people in a developing economy, so this may be one of the most important measures of development, and it is a better measure than landlines **a** which are not so versatile owing to the need for a wider infrastructure.

🅔 **6/6 marks awarded.** The mobile phone measure is perfectly acceptable and well explained. **a** The student attempts to evaluate by saying it is has advantages relative to another measure: that is, prioritisation with justification.

*(c) One benefit of growth is that incomes are rising, and if incomes are rising, people are likely to have higher standards of living. Economic growth is one of the six macroeconomic objectives of governments, and growth has two main causes. The causes of growth **a** are a shift to the right in the *AD* and a shift to the right in the *AS*. *AD* might rise because consumption, investment, government spending or exports have risen, or because saving, taxes or imports have fallen. There is a multiplier effect. *AS* might rise because there is a fall in investment, a fall in production costs such as wages, or a rise in the exchange rate making imports cheaper.

The benefits of growth ʙ for consumers are that they can buy more goods and services with their higher incomes, or they could have longer holidays and shorter working hours. Benefits for the government are that it receives higher tax revenue (this assumes that the tax thresholds remain the same) and this means that it is easier for the government to make income distribution more equal by the 'Robin Hood' process of taxing the rich to give to the poor. Firms also benefit because they have higher profits (because they sell more) and even the environment might improve because rich countries that have signed the Kyoto agreement of 1997 are committed to using cleaner and greener methods of production, and these methods cost money which the increased income from the growth can pay for through an increase in tax revenues.

The costs of growth are the environmental damage. More production means more pollution and depletion of natural resources. Also, income distribution might not get better because it tends to be the rich people who get richer quicker when the economy is growing, whereas people like cleaners get paid the same. Also, higher incomes usually involve longer workings hours, not shorter ones.

ⓔ **12/30 marks awarded. a** This student has made a classic error in starting with the *causes* rather than the *effects* of growth. While this does not lose the student any marks, nor does it gain any, and there is an opportunity cost in that less time can be devoted to relevant material.

b The student has listed the standard points for and against the benefits and costs of growth, but the evaluation is limited. It is clear from the answer that there are two sides to every point, but it would be better to discuss the advantages and disadvantages of each point in turn and come to a reasoned conclusion.

An important evaluation point that could be made is that the effects might be different in the short run and the long run. For example, although economic growth often makes income distribution worse in the short run, these incomes might even out over time as the 'rich' spend their money, with multiplier effects. A second evaluation point might be that the effect on the environment might be difficult to measure, and it depends on whether the growth is based in the industrial or services sector. In the latter case, the environmental aspects will not be so significant.

To summarise, the student would score well on analysis marks but is lacking application and evaluation.

Total score: 49/80 = grade C

Question 2 **Food and oil prices**

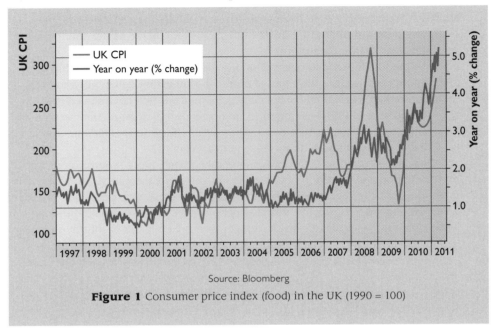

Source: Bloomberg

Figure 1 Consumer price index (food) in the UK (1990 = 100)

Table 1 Oil price changes in pounds and dollars (Brent crude)

Currency	Percentage change on previous month				
	2007				**2008**
	Sep	**Oct**	**Nov**	**Dec**	**Jan**
Pounds	8.2	5.9	10.9	1.2	3.1
Dollars	8.6	7.3	12.3	−1.5	0.9

Source: **www.bankofengland.co.uk**

(a) Refer to Figure 1.

(i) Using Figure 1, calculate the percentage change in the food price index between January 2008 and January 2011. (4 marks)

The question requires you to read the scales accurately and perform a percentage change calculation. It is important to avoid using the wrong scale and to remember which is the **original** figure for the percentage change formula.

(ii) Assess the likely impact on UK income distribution when food prices rise. (12 marks)

For income distribution questions, you must identify groups of people and how they are affected in terms of the proportion of their income being spent on food

Edexcel AS Economics

(b) Making reference to Table 1:

   (i) **Explain what happened to oil prices in December 2007 in both pounds and dollars.** (4 marks)

ⓔ Use the data carefully.

   (ii) **Outline one likely reason for this difference.** (4 marks)

ⓔ The reason must be based on the relative value of the currencies.

   (iii) **With the aid of an aggregate demand and supply diagram, analyse the likely impact on the UK's real output and price level of the trend in oil prices over the period from July 2007 to January 2008.** (16 marks)

ⓔ Oil prices affect *AD* through *X* and *M* (the UK is a net importer) and through *AS* because oil is a major production cost.

(c) Apart from food and oil prices, explain two factors that the Bank of England's Monetary Policy Committee considers when it makes its interest rate decision. (10 marks)

ⓔ Factors could include house prices, wages and productivity, but the list is enormous. Avoid soft arguments such as those saying that the MPC considers current interest rates or inflation when making its decision. It is a weak argument to say that you look at inflation to explain what is going to happen to inflation, just as you would not look at the weather now to see what the weather is going to be like. If you look at the current situation and can make inferences from it — for example, by observing a trend — then this would be a valid argument. But on its own it is not convincing to the examiner. Similarly, saying that you look at interest rates to decide what is going to happen to inflation is like saying a person looks at how strong their sun cream is to see what the weather will be. Sun cream is used to prevent the adverse effects of the weather; in the same way, the interest rate is used to prevent the worst repercussions of inflation. There are much easier ways to approach this question, by looking at the **causes** of inflation (such as wage pressures).

*(d)Discuss the likely effects on the price level in the UK if interest rates are raised. Consider the impact on the economy of a change in the exchange rate in your answer. (30 marks)

ⓔ This is a question about tight monetary policy: that is, raising interest rates. The aim is to decrease inflationary pressures by suppressing aggregate demand. The transmission mechanisms by which interest rate changes impact upon *AD* include changes in consumption and investment and changes to net trade. The effect on net trade may occur because the exchange rate changes. Remember that changes in the interest rate and the exchange rate tend to happen in the same direction — if the interest rate rises, so does the exchange rate.

Student Answer

(a) (i) (275 –175) = 100%

ⓔ **1/4 marks awarded.** The student has selected the correct years and read the data accurately from the graph, but the formula for percentage change is always (change/original) × 100, which in this case is (275 − 175/175) × 100 = 57.1%. Remember to show the sign if it is a fall.

> **(ii)** Everybody needs food and rich people probably spend more on food than poor people, so I would guess that income distribution doesn't change much, if it improves at all. **a** However, it depends which food gets more expensive. If it's fast food it might affect poor people more, but if it's caviar it would affect rich people more.

ⓔ **5/12 marks a** It would be wise to mention the proportion of income spent, not the absolute values. Rising food prices mean that lower-income groups have less money to spend after food has been paid for. However, the gross income remains unaffected unless you want to argue that rising food prices somehow reduce the gross income of lower-income groups; it would be better to argue in the evaluation that the income distribution changes *after* food costs have been taken into account.

From the brevity of the answer it is clear that the student is on unsure ground. If you are uncertain, it is unwise to tell the examiner you are guessing; instead, follow through your ideas with reasons as far as you can. This is an evaluative question because more than one answer can be given. The student clearly recognises this and gains marks for attempting to evaluate. Altogether on the paper there are 20 evaluation marks: two questions with 4 marks each, and the essay at the end with 12 marks.

(b) (i) In pounds they rose by 1.2% but in dollars they fell by 1.5%.

ⓔ **4/4 marks awarded.** Data are selected correctly and the answer makes it clear that one is rising and one is falling. Remember to refer to the minus signs as 'falling'.

> **(ii)** Obviously the pound got stronger.

ⓔ **1/4 marks awarded.** If something is 'obvious', it usually follows that it is not worth asking a question about. It is true that the pound has probably gained in strength against the dollar, but it might be that the dollar fell, or the dollar and the pound fell with the dollar falling faster. The key point is that the exchange rate between the pound and the dollar has strengthened and the dollar will buy fewer units of oil. For 2 marks there needs to be reference to the exchange rate, not just the pound, and for the other 2 marks there must be some reference to the data. It is sensible to back up your reasoning with a simple calculation: for example, £1 = $2 falling to £1 = $1.50 means that UK consumers will not be able to buy as many US goods with the same number of pounds. You could add a simple picture here, such as US wine bottles with price tags on.

(iii) The UK is a net importer of food and oil. Although we produce both, we buy more in value terms from abroad than we export. When prices of these commodities go up, the response by consumers is very small — in other words there is low price-elasticity of demand. When PED is less than 1, a rise in prices means that total expenditure rises, so when the prices of these goods go up, total expenditure on imports rises. Imports are a component of *AD* (aggregate demand) and therefore *AD* falls. This effect is made more extreme by the multiplier effect. **a**

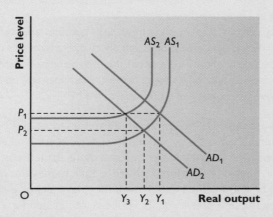

b

The increase in commodity prices also affects aggregate supply, which in a sense is the cost of production. All producers need oil and food in the UK and therefore all firms' costs will rise, therefore *AS* shifts to the left, prices rise and output falls.

Overall the price effects might outweigh each other, but the output effects will reinforce each other (return to P_1), and we would expect a fall or a slowdown in real output Y_3.

e 16/16 marks awarded. This answer includes **a** the multiplier and **b** an accurate diagram, and covers both the *AD* and *AS* sides of the case. Most answers will give only the *AS* side and this one stands out as far better than the average. No evaluation is required, so this earns full marks.

(c) First factor: The MPC (Monetary Policy Committee) takes into account the current account of the balance of payments. If there is a deficit such as the one the UK is currently experiencing (£45 billion) this is a sign that the UK economy is spending more than it is selling abroad, and it might be that the pound will fall in the future, which is inflationary (imports become more expensive). However, the deficit itself is not inflationary and therefore the MPC is unlikely to be worried directly by a deficit. In fact, if $X - M$ is less than zero there is a negative effect on *AD*, which *reduces* inflationary pressure.

e 5/5 marks awarded. This is an ideal answer. The current account is one of the many thousands of factors looked at by the Monetary Policy Committee when making its interest rate decision. A deficit may mean that inflation will not hit the target. The answer stresses the role of the MPC and the inflation target, and gives real-world evidence.

Second factor: The MPC looks very carefully at house prices. If house prices are falling, as they were during the autumn of 2007, this can mean that there is a negative wealth effect. **a** In the USA this triggered a credit crunch, and interest rates have had to fall dramatically to try to keep demand up. **b** If demand is falling there will be unemployment. **c**

🄴 **3/5 marks awarded. a** Wealth effects are the effects on spending (or similar) when asset values change. **b** Interest rates are cut to stimulate spending and investment in an economy. **c** However, there may be a time lag. Unemployment is a lagging indicator, meaning that it tends to worsen after the worst of a recession is over

The student adopts a common approach to this type of question, and starts off well. By focusing on some real data and the concept of wealth effects, the answer hits on an important area of concern for the Monetary Policy Committee. But then no link is made to inflation, and instead the answer heads off to talk about unemployment, which may well be an important consideration for the government but is of no concern to the MPC.

*(d) If interest rates are raised there will be an impact on most of the components of aggregate demand, $C + I + G + (X - M)$. First we look at consumption (C). C falls for many reasons. One is that savings become more attractive and loans become more expensive. People will be less inclined to take money out of savings to spend, and will be less inclined to borrow if they have a choice about their spending. For example, a person might choose to delay buying a car. Also people will find things bought on hire purchase will have higher monthly instalments, so they will be less inclined to borrow in this way. Also C falls because mortgage interest payments will increase so people will have less money left over to buy goods and services. Also people may feel less confident about the economy so they might rein back their spending plans. This would be especially true for people who have their own businesses and expect sales to fall.

Secondly, investment will also fall when interest rates rise. This is because the interest rate is the cost of borrowing money for investment, and only very profitable projects will be worth taking the risk of investing in when interest rates are too high.

Thirdly, $X - M$ will be likely to fall. This is for two reasons. The first is that we will export less (as firms face higher interest rates there are increased production costs) and imports will fall (we will suck in fewer imports because our spending is down). The second reason is that the pound is likely to rise. This is because hot money will be attracted to the pound as sterling bank accounts will be earning higher returns. With a 'Strong Pound Imports are Cheap and Exports are Dear' (SPICED). This means that M will rise and X will fall, so AD will fall. This is made even more pronounced because of the multiplier.

AD falls meaning prices will fall and output will fall. **a**

The extent of the impact on the price levels depends on where on the *AS* curve the *AD* crosses. If *AS* is very inelastic (the steep part), the impact on the price level will be very large. The economy will have very little spare capacity and there will be strong pressures to increase prices. A rise in the interest rate will relieve much of the pressure on prices as people stop spending, and the price level will fall significantly. However if the *AD* crosses the more elastic part of the *AS* curve, there will be little effect on prices and a large effect on the level of output and probably employment in the country. Raising interest rates will just bring more gloom in an economy where there is a lot of spare capacity already, and people deciding to spend less will cause further stagnation in the economy. **b**

Another evaluation point is that the interest rate impact does not always happen immediately. Many people have fixed rate mortgages, and even if mortgage interest payments do change, the mortgage holder might not react straight away. It is the same with the exchange rate. Even if the pound gets stronger, it probably won't make people stop buying things from the UK. If foreign tourists have booked their holidays already, they won't cancel if the pound gets stronger. They just might think more carefully about where they go in the future. This is a time lag, and it depends on the price elasticity of demand for exports and imports. **c**

⊜ 28/30 marks awarded. An excellent analysis (18/18). **a** There are just a couple of points to note on the analysis side: the SPICED acronym is really useful for you to remember the effect of a change in the exchange rate, but you don't want to tell the examiner about it. Secondly, the first point about $(X - M)$, with X falling and M rising due to changes in spending in the UK, is really a repeat of the argument about C, so it would have been better just to do the analysis concerning the change in the exchange rate, as indicated in the question.

The evaluation marks are **b** 6/6 and **c** 4/6. There is one very good piece of evaluation followed by a slightly less developed attempt. The student might have offered a third point: for example, that the pound is influenced by many things apart from the interest rates, or that relative interest rates are important, so the Fed and ECB rates need to be taken into account. Also in evaluation, if interest rates rise and *AD* slows, firms in the UK might look for new export markets to keep sales figures buoyant, so the balance of payments might not worsen as much. Then three pieces of evaluation could be rewarded 4 + 4 + 4 and full marks would be awarded overall.

Overall, despite some very uncertain areas in the question as a whole, the student gets to an A by making sure that the longer answers pull up the grade.

Total score: 63/80 = grade A

Question 3 Income and wealth

Table 1 House prices in the UK

	Average house price	Index	Monthly change (%)	Annual change (%)
January 2008	£229,625	233.8	0.1	6.5
December 2007	£229,496	233.7	−0.2	7.4
November 2007	£230,031	234.2	−0.1	8.9
October 2007	£230,284	234.5	0.6	9.8

Source: **www.bankofengland.co.uk**

Extract 1

The international economy and UK GDP growth

International economic prospects have deteriorated since the last November inflation report. In the United States GDP growth fell sharply, the labour market weakened and the weakness in the housing market appeared to be spreading to other parts of the economy. As a result the Federal Reserve in the USA reduced official interest rates substantially. In the euro area business surveys pointed to some slowing in output growth from its recent healthy figures. In contrast, the emerging market economies of Asia continued to expand robustly.

Overall, the Committee expects a modest slowing in the growth of the main UK export markets. That is offset by the depreciation of sterling, which can be expected to boost UK competitiveness.

Consequently net trade is expected to add to GDP growth over the next few years, contrary to the experience over much of the past decade.

GDP growth moderated to 0.6% in the period October to December 2007 according to preliminary estimates, with the slowdown most significant in the financial and retail sectors. Business surveys and reports from the Bank's regional Agents point to a further modest slowdown in activity in early 2008.

Adapted from Bank of England, Inflation Report, February 2008, **www.bankofengland.co.uk**

(a) (i) Describe what happened to house prices in December 2007.   (4 marks)

ⓔ Remember that a minus sign in any data is very interesting to economists. It means that something has fallen in value.

(ii) Outline the likely impact of this change in house prices on consumer expenditure. Refer to the *wealth effect* in your answer.   (6 marks)

ⓔ A wealth effect is when a change in asset values affects income or spending. It can be positive or negative depending what has happened to asset prices.

Edexcel AS Economics

(iii) **With reference to the information provided, evaluate the likely effects on the UK price level and equilibrium real output of the changes in incomes in the international economy.** (12 marks)

(e) For questions that ask about the impact on the price level and real output, you must draw an *AD/AS* diagram. A worldwide recession is likely to make aggregate demand fall as exports decrease, or at least rise more slowly.

(b) (i) **With reference to Extract I, explain what is meant by the term *injection*.** (6 marks)

(e) There are three injections into the circular flow: *I*, *G* and *X*. Remember that consumption is not an injection.

(ii) **Outline the mechanism by which a change in an injection can have a greater impact on total incomes in an economy.** (10 marks)

(e) This is a question about the multiplier. There is no need to evaluate, but make sure that you earn the marks by spelling out the process clearly.

(c) **Discuss the likely effect on the price level in the UK when interest rates fall in the USA.** (12 marks)

(e) The transmission mechanism will be via *X* and *M*. Think about what happens when incomes in the USA start rising.

*(d) **To what extent is it likely that policies intended to increase economic growth will conflict with the working of other government policies?** (30 marks)

(e) For the marking structure of your answer, refer to Question I(c), p. 55. Remember that you need to think of a maximum of only three conflicts and focus on policies not objectives.

Student Answer

(a) (i) They rose by 7.4%.

(e) **0/4 marks awarded.** The student was probably rushing and misread the data: 7.4% is the change between December 2006 and December 2007, but the change over the *month* was a *fall* of 0.2%.

(ii) When house prices go up, consumer expenditure goes up. **a** This is because housing in the UK is the major form of asset held by consumers — almost half of everything they own. When the value of assets goes up, people holding them tend to feel better off, and therefore spend more. This is called a wealth effect. Rising house prices also mean that people can take out increased loans based on the increased value of their property, a process called equity release, and this again means that consumer expenditure may increase.

6/6 marks awarded. a Although the student got the direction wrong for the change in house prices, he or she is not penalised again in this part of the question. This answer shows a good understanding of wealth effects (3/3) and gives two reasons why house price rises would lead to more spending. Another approach would be to refer to increased consumer confidence.

(iii) In the passage it says that the euro area and the USA are experiencing a slowdown in incomes, whereas Asian economies are growing and the overall impact is that UK exports are rising, albeit at a slowing rate. Increases in net exports will boost the circular flow in the UK, which shifts the AD to the right.

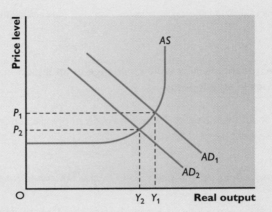

Price levels rise and output rises. However, the passage also states that the value of sterling is falling which 'can be expected to boost UK competitiveness', so although exports are rising more slowly, the fall in the value of the pound will make exports increasingly cheap relative to other goods and services in the international economy, and imports relatively expensive. This might mean that AD increases at a faster rate. It all depends on the price-elasticity of demand for exports and imports. **b**

8/12 marks awarded. This succinct answer makes good use of the passage and provides clear analytical observations. **a** However, in the diagram the AD shift is shown in the wrong direction and this means that the four easy diagram marks are missed. **b** The evaluation is valid, but another point that could have been mentioned is that the UK does most of its trade (73%) with the euro area and this area will therefore have the most significant impact on the level of exports from the UK.

(b) (i) An injection is an input into the circular flow of income. Examples are investment, government spending and exports. When these rise, the circular flow of income rises because they are exogenous: that is, from outside the system.

4/6 marks awarded. This is a textbook explanation of the term. However, there is no reference to Extract 1, where the report refers to exports.

(ii) The multiplier is a formula that relates an initial change in spending to the total change in spending that will result. A change in an injection has multiplier effects. When, for example, exports increase there is a flow of money into the economy which is in a sense new money. It will become an income for the exporting firm which will then spend this money on paying the factors of production, for example wages. The workers who earn this money may spend it which means the money becomes someone else's income. These knock-on effects in the economy of a change in income will have a greatly magnified effect on incomes as a whole. The amount by which a change in the injection has a final impact depends on the size of the leakages. The leakages are savings, tax and imports. These take money out of the flow and reduce the multiplier effect. The bigger the leakages, the smaller the multiplier. Eventually the multiplier process dies out as the extra spending of the economy leaks away.

ⓔ **10/10 marks awarded.** While the prose is not sophisticated, the ideas are expressed clearly and the mechanics of the multiplier are delivered effectively.

(c) When interest rates fall in the USA people in the USA will feel better off and will start spending more. One reason is because mortgage repayments will fall and they will have more money to spend on goods and services, some of which might be the UK's exports. Consumer spending might also rise because the Americans will save less and feel more confident about taking out loans. Therefore, American firms will find they can sell goods and services more easily in the USA and the incentive to sell goods and services to the UK will not be so strong. Therefore the UK will experience a rise in exports and a fall in imports. This will increase *AD*, so price levels in the UK will rise. Also, when interest rates fall in the USA the dollar will fall in value. This effectively means that the pound is stronger, and this means that the UK will find it more difficult to export and easier to import. These effects might outweigh each other, although I think the second argument is stronger. a

ⓔ **10/12 marks awarded.** The analysis is secure and there is an attempt at evaluation by saying that 'effects might outweigh each other' and it depends on which is greater. a However, when students use the personal pronoun and say 'I think…', it does little to convince the examiner; it would be better to spell out reasons why one effect might be greater than another.

***(d)** Policies intended to increase growth can be reflationary demand-side policies such as monetary and fiscal policy, or supply-side policies. Fiscal policy might be used to increase aggregate demand by increasing government spending (*G*) or cutting taxation (*T*). Monetary policy can be used to increase growth by cutting interest rates, although in the UK the Monetary Policy Committee does not aim to increase growth, it rather allows growth to occur by cutting interest rates when inflation falls below target. These shift *AD* to the right, and the effect on national income is magnified by the multiplier effect.

These policies are likely to conflict with the working of policies to improve the environment. Green taxes can be used to try to change the way people use goods and services with a high carbon use. Cutting taxes generally would mean that people have more money to drive large cars and fly to foreign countries for their holidays. The higher people's incomes become with economic growth, the less sensitive they are to green taxes. So even if cutting taxes in other areas outweighs the green taxes, the green taxes themselves will not have a very powerful environmental impact as the economy grows.

Supply-side policies are any action by the authorities to try to increase competition, incentives and the flexibility of the workforce. In the past they have included privatisation and deregulation, but they can also include tax cuts and legislation to reduce the power of the trade unions or cutting the national minimum wage. The aim is to shift the aggregate supply curve to the right. Costs will fall in the economy, and the equilibrium will occur at a higher rate of GDP.

However, supply-side policies do have side-effects which might conflict with the workings of other government policies. For example, reducing the power of trade unions or cutting the national minimum wage is unlikely to improve the distribution of income. But in other ways the supply-side policies might improve the working of other policies such as monetary policy. As costs fall in the economy, this will dampen inflationary pressures. And cutting taxes to improve incentives has a similar effect to expansionary fiscal policy.

ⓔ **26/30 marks awarded.** This answer covers the main policies effectively, and there are two good attempts at evaluation. The answer would gain full marks with the inclusion of a diagram showing how these policies affect price levels and real output, or the equivalent written explanation. Without these, the final 4 marks were not earned.

Total score: 64/80 = grade A

Question 4 **Conflicts between fiscal policy and other government policy**

Extract 1

George Osborne vows to 'put fuel into the tank of the British economy' in March 2011 Budget

Fuel duty cut by 1p and fuel duty escalator scrapped

Corporation tax cut by 2p – not 1p as expected

Annual growth forecast revised down from 2.1% to 1.7%

National insurance and income tax may be merged

George Osborne has levied a £2bn windfall tax on Britain's North Sea oil companies to pay for a cut in petrol duties for motorists struggling because of the soaring price of crude oil on global markets. The chancellor said he wanted his budget to 'put fuel into the tank of the British economy'. He told the Commons he was scrapping the previous Labour government's plans for automatic above-inflation increases in fuel duties and would instead be cutting 1p a litre from forecourt prices from tonight. In the sort of flourish that was Gordon Brown's trademark at the end of his budgets, Osborne announced the fuel duty cut at the climax of a speech built around the theme of boosting growth and rebalancing the economy. The cost of 'filling up a family car such as a Ford Focus has increased by £10', he said, and he wanted to do something to help.

He said he was cutting corporation tax (tax on firms' profits) by 2p in the pound this year rather than the 1p reduction previously planned, and announced a shake-up of planning laws and the removal of hundreds of regulations in an attempt to stimulate enterprise.

However, the Labour leader, Ed Miliband, said Osborne's claim to have delivered a budget for growth was undermined by a cut in the growth forecast for 2011 from 2.1% to 1.7%.

Source: **www.guardian.co.uk/uk/2011/mar/23/george-osborne-fuel-tank-british-economy**
© Guardian News and Media Ltd

Every major budget has a defining moment. For most of the media it was the Ford Focus fuel cut, as the only headline worth noting in a pretty boring budget. But there was a much more telling moment, which says everything you need to know about this government's guiding principles. Having hammered the poorest by cutting £18bn from welfare payments, driven up unemployment with its public sector cuts — after it was starting to fall last summer — and given all working people pay freezes, after-inflation wage cuts and pension contribution hikes, George Osborne's tour de force was a handout to big business, with a 2p corporation tax cut. 'Britain', he proudly proclaimed, 'is open for business.'

Source: **www.guardian.co.uk/commentisfree/2011/mar/24/**
© Guardian News and Media Ltd

Extract 2

Using the Budget to make it easy to go green

Friends of the Earth has made its expectations clear in its demands for a green Budget. It outlined a variety of measures the government must adopt to help the UK to develop a low-carbon economy, including a windfall tax on producers of energy and a £10 billion tax shift programme raising taxes on pollution (including a fuel escalator tax) and cutting taxes on income.

Friends of the Earth's Economics Co-ordinator Simon Bullock said: 'Carbon dioxide emissions just keep on rising. We've had enough of half measures and green spin. The Chancellor must put climate change at the heart of the Budget and make it cheaper and easier for people to go green.'

Adapted from Friends of the Earth website, **www.foe.co.uk**

(a) Explain what is meant by the term 'fiscal policy'. (6 marks)

ⓔ Apart from referring to G and T, you must use the data and put fiscal policy in the context of the government's budget.

(b) With reference to Extract I:

(i) Using an appropriate diagram, analyse how the cut in tax on firms' profits outlined in the extract may be used to 'kick start the economy'. (16 marks)

ⓔ Cutting taxes on firms is a supply-side policy aimed at shifting AS to the right.

(ii) Assess the likely impact on the distribution of income in the UK which will result from the tax changes. (14 marks)

ⓔ For any income distribution question you must identify groups that are affected, for example employees and students on fixed incomes.

(c) With reference to Extracts I and 2, examine one way in which fiscal policy may be used to incorporate environmental goals. (14 marks)

ⓔ Governments can use both spending patterns and appropriate taxes in order to change the way consumers and firms have an impact on the environment. For example, they can cut taxes on greener fuels, or subsidise the installation of solar energy-generating equipment.

*(d) Discuss the likely effect of changes in fiscal policy for the decisions on monetary policy made by the Monetary Policy Committee. Consider both the short and the long run in your response. (30 marks)

ⓔ When a government operates a loose fiscal policy, the shortfall in tax revenue has to be found by raising funds in the money markets. This demand for funds puts an upward pressure on interest rates, but in the long run if the fiscal policy is effective in creating jobs and encouraging growth, the effects on monetary policy could be reversed.

Student answer

(a) Fiscal policy is the government's manipulation of its spending (*G*) and taxation (*T*) in order to affect aggregate demand. Fiscal policy decisions are made by the government in the budget in March, although some further changes are often made in the autumn in the Pre-Budget Report. Fiscal policy can be used to achieve a variety of policy objectives, mainly economic growth, employment, and the distribution of income. Increasingly, in the views of some economists, fiscal policy has included 'green taxes' as a means to prevent further environmental problems.

If government spending is increased relative to taxation, then fiscal policy is said to be expansionary and *AD* shifts to the right. If government spending is increased at a slower rate than taxation, then fiscal policy is said to be contractionary. **a** In Extract 1 there are references to a cut in fuel taxes and in corporation tax of 2%.

ⓔ **6/6 marks awarded. a** Accurate answers such as this earn full marks, including data marks.

(b) (i) Cutting taxes in the economy implies that the government is aiming to increase output and spending. This can be shown by a movement to the right of *AD* on the real output axis.

The increase in government spending of £2.7 billion will increase aggregate demand. Price levels will increase and output will increase. There will be a multiplier effect, which is the knock-on effect when an injection such as *G* increases while *T* stays constant.

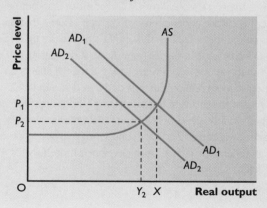

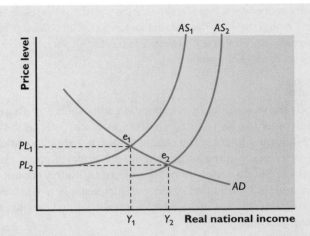

There will also be an impact on the supply side of the economy. If people are paying less tax there will be an incentive to work harder for those already in work, and those who are not in the workforce (the economically inactive) will have an increased incentive to join the workforce. As the workforce increases, wages will be bid downwards and the economy becomes more competitive. **a** However, there is not likely to be much change in the short run, as profit taxes will not have much impact on firms if demand is so low that they are not making significant profit, and the change in profit tax might be too small to have much effect. The falls in aggregate demand thanks to cuts in the public sector and cuts in benefits will more than likely outweigh any increases in supply that result from the cuts in taxes because firms are unlikely to increase investment in a time of economic uncertainty.

ⓔ **10/16 marks awarded.** The analysis is weak because on the demand side there is not likely to be a significant increase — there are several cuts in G that more than outweigh any fall in T. Just because the government is cutting expenditure, you cannot assume that taxes will rise, or even fall. The supply side is considered well. The shift in AD is not correctly applied in the diagram because the answer says AD increases, but the diagram shows it decreasing. It would also be better to incorporate both shifts on one diagram to show the overall effects on output, with both of the shifts increasing the equilibrium real output. It is odd that different labels are used on the horizontal axis for what is meant to represent the same thing. Therefore, full marks would not be earned for the diagrams; they would receive only 1 out of the 4 marks available. **a** The student receives 4/4 evaluation marks, awarded as 2 + 2 for considering magnitude issues and outweighing factors. Alternatively, one argument could have been developed more fully for 4 marks.

(b) (ii) In general a tax windfall like this is likely to help lower income groups by a larger proportion than higher income groups. Therefore the distribution of income will 'improve' in the sense that inequalities are reduced. However, this masks some of the picture.

In Extract 1 it is stated that standard rate tax payers will gain by £120 a year, but this will not affect top rate taxpayers. Actually this is wrong, because top rate taxpayers do also pay standard rate tax on some of their income. While it will affect the distribution of income (lower income groups will see a higher proportional benefit) it is not exactly as the author makes out. Furthermore, at the other end of the income distribution, people who don't have any work at all will not gain the £120 and therefore the distribution of income will widen.

ⓔ **14/14 marks awarded.** The analysis is secure because two groups are identified and the relative change in income for these groups is described. The evaluation is also highly awarded because the student pulls out a major inaccuracy in the data. Clearly top rate taxpayers will get the £120 benefit too. However, this level of analysis is not expected in AS Unit 2, so while the marks will be awarded the point is unlikely to appear on the official mark scheme. Other ways to evaluate would be to say that the increased government borrowing will have to be paid back at some point, and it is not clear which part of the population will pay that. In addition, other things are not equal. Lower income taxes might attract more investment from abroad, which might mean more job opportunities for people in Britain. More demand for workers will make wages rise.

(c) Green taxes can be used as part of fiscal policy. This is where the main aim of the policy is not to change *AD* but to change the way in which spending occurs so that carbon dioxide emissions are reduced. One obvious way to do this is to increase the tax on petrol. Of course no one likes paying more, but the net effect on consumer disposable income need not change overall because the government could spend more on public services such as transport. In Extract 2 this is called a '£10 billion tax shift programme', and the emphasis is on changing the way in which taxes are imposed and not the overall tax burden. **a**

In my view the cost of petrol is already far too high, **b** and most of the journeys that are made are necessary to the way our economy works. In other words, demand is price inelastic because the public services are total rubbish. **c** Trains are overcrowded and buses only go along the main, congested routes and never at times to suit demand. If the private sector was running the transport system it might not be any better, but I can't see how throwing money at the public sector is going to help. You can't have more trains running on the Underground; it's already at full capacity. Transport is the main thing stifling productivity growth in the UK, and green taxes are not going to help.

ⓔ **10/14 marks awarded. a** The good thing about this answer is that it uses the passage, describes how green taxes would work, and goes on to evaluate. **b** The bad thing is that the comments are rather over-enthusiastic in rhetoric, and measured analysis is the opportunity cost here. **c** Rather than using words such as 'rubbish' and 'of course', more effort could be put into offering a viable solution.

(d) The MPC considers an enormous range of data when coming to a decision on the interest rate. It looks at pressures in the labour market, housing market, commodity prices, external exchange and the global economy, to name but a few. The fiscal stance is also of great interest to the MPC. If the government is seen as operating a loose fiscal policy as outlined in Extract 1, the MPC might consider the impact on the real side of the economy and on the money markets. Government spending has to be financed and if it is not going to be financed by taxation then the money has to come from somewhere. In this case it is by borrowing. It is the extent to which borrowing affects inflationary pressures which is of concern to the MPC. The MPC has only one objective: to maintain the inflation target. Therefore any softness by the government in its fiscal policy is likely to be compensated for by tight monetary policy — that is a raising of interest rates.

The borrowing can have two very different effects on inflationary pressures. If there is spare capacity in the economy then expansionary fiscal policy can cause some increased growth without damaging inflationary pressures. If there is no spare capacity — that is, full employment — then there will be inflation. This can be shown using an *AS* curve, and as the elasticity falls (the *AS* curve gets steeper), the inflationary pressures increase. a

There is a similar set of opposites in the money markets. If there is plenty of credit around then extra government borrowing will not have much effect on the cost of credit. But in times of the 'credit crunch' when it is hard to get loans and interbank loans are at high interest rates then increased borrowing will crowd out the market. In this case, government expansion will not be inflationary, and will merely tighten the monetary side of the economy.

In conclusion, it is difficult to say how the MPC will react to expansionary fiscal policy. It depends entirely on the context. If there is spare capacity in the economy and there is plenty of available credit then it is unlikely to react. But in the case where bottlenecks are appearing and prices are edging upwards, the MPC might raise rates. If the money market is short of credit, however, this might not be needed as increased cost of credit will in itself control aggregate demand and therefore restrain inflationary pressures.

ⓔ **28/30 marks awarded.** This is a sophisticated response, on what is probably the most challenging part of the specification. a The only noticeable weakness is the absence of a diagram, although the shape of the *AS* curve is described well. A simple sketch to illustrate the bottlenecks in supply would earn 4/4 diagram marks rather than the 2 marks earned from describing it.

Total score: 68/80 = grade A

Knowledge check answers

1 Increases in GDP are growth.

2 Real values have the effects of inflation removed.

3 Developing countries can grow more quickly because they are starting from a lower base — so the same input of £100m into a diamond refinery would have a larger percentage impact on growth figures in Botswana than in the UK.

4 An index is used to make comparisons over time and between countries. A base year is chosen and given the value 100, and changes are shown as percentage changes relative to the base year.

5 The price survey tells us the change in prices for each good and service that is bought, and the expenditure survey shows us the proportion spent on each item, so that we can weight the price changes in terms of their importance to us as consumers.

6 No — they exclude the cost of mortgage interest repayments. There are not any measures of inflation which include the mortgage itself, because the mortgage debt does not change with inflation. If anything, mortgages decrease in real terms in times of inflation.

7 Housing costs are not included in the CPI measure, used by many other countries. Also housing costs include mortgage interest rates which usually change when interest rates change, so raising interest rates (meant to reduce inflation) will in the short term make the rate of inflation higher if housing costs are included.

8 To do this it might help to know the deficiencies of each measure. For example, if you cannot claim JSA when you have a high level of savings, ILO unemployment will rise more quickly than the claimant count as people of all types, with various levels of savings, lose their jobs in a recession.

9 The focus of the answer should be on the two types of survey involved, and there is opportunity cost involved in defining terms that are not required by the question. A weighted basket of goods, a price survey, an index and a base year should all form part of your answer.

10 New immigrants will fill jobs that people in the UK either cannot or do not want to fill, increasing employment levels (but not necessarily employment rates). Some immigrants might displace UK workers, so UK workers might become unemployed. In addition, family might accompany working immigrants in the hope of finding work, and these will eventually be able to claim unemployment status.

11 The claimant count is the number of people who actually receive JSA. There are many who do not actually claim it, for various reasons (they might not be out of work for a very long time, for example). These do not register in the statistics for the unemployed by this method, but they could be picked up by the ILO method.

12 They are 'economically inactive' because they might be students or looking after children or carrying out other functions in the home.

13 The level is the total number employed, while the rate is the total number employed relative to the number of people of working age.

14 Yes. The easiest way to decide whether or not something is an import is to look at the direction of the money flow. If money is leaving the country, the trade is an import.

15 If the figure is positive, the country excels in education and health relative to incomes, and vice versa for a negative outcome.

16 AIDS does have stark and painful consequences not just for the sufferer, but for dependants. However, it is very difficult to measure because it is an immune deficiency, and sufferers' actual cause of death is another disease or problem. There is also social stigma to reporting AIDS.

17 Growth measures incomes, while development measures the quality of life, distribution of incomes and access to resources.

18 No. The injections are investment, government spending and exports.

19 No. An increase in house prices tends to make people spend more, for two reasons. One is that they feel more confident. A second is that they can take out loans using the increased value of their house as collateral — a process known as mortgage equity withdrawal.

20 No. People tend to consume about the same in total at lower prices, although they get more for their money. That is, C is roughly constant in money terms at various price levels.

21 It tends to rise because of the wealth effect.

22 No. If there is no spare capacity in the economy, the AS curve will be vertical, and classical economists draw the AS curve as entirely vertical in the long-run situation. Keynesians draw the AS curve as a combination of horizontal, (spare capacity), upward sloping (some bottlenecks) and vertical (full capacity). Alternatively, for simplicity, you can draw a gently upward-sloping AS curve for the short run, and vertical or very steep AS curves for the long run.

23 A cut in education spending decreases AD (short term) and AS (long term).

24 A rise in interest rates cuts AD (short term) and AS (short-term increases in the cost of borrowing, and long-term fall in investment).

25 An increase in productivity relative to EU/US: an increase in AD (as X rises and M falls, although only in the long term as price elasticity of demand is likely to be low in the short run) and fall in AS if the relative cost of imports rises (short term) but an increase in AS if there is more investment from abroad (long term).

26 Actual growth can be defined as an increase in real GDP and potential growth as an increase in capacity in the economy.

27 This is not true if the increase is in potential growth, and not necessarily true if the increase is in actual growth. It depends on the availability of spare resources: that is, an output gap.

28 There are many arguments on both sides. Increasing benefits reduces poverty and inequality; or costs of living are rising so benefits should rise or the benefits will fall in real terms. Cutting benefits might make the unemployed more eager to get back to work as they cannot sustain living standards while out of work; or consider the opportunity cost of benefits; or consider the fiscal policy implications, e.g. taxes might have to rise, which might lead to disincentives in other parts of the labour market.

29 If there is a shortage of a particular type of worker, then higher wages will need to be offered to attract workers from other jobs. As wages rise for some jobs, and spending more generally increases, other wages and prices will be bid upwards.

30 It makes a country's exports relatively cheap and imports relatively expensive. Remember, though, that the pattern of demand might not change immediately.

31 • Industrialisation, e.g. pollution, congestion.
 • What about if the growth is in the service sector?
 • Depletion of natural resources.

- More efficient use of resources.
- Higher incomes mean more foreign travel, usually by air, increasing carbon emissions.
- Higher government revenues from taxation mean there is more money to clean up and introduce carbon capping schemes, or carbon offsetting.

32

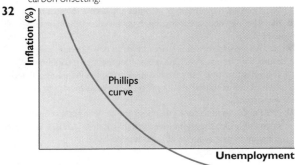

33 In terms of the 'real economy' (actual goods and services), there are demand pressures (increases in *AD*) and cost pressures (decreases in *AS*). There is also the monetary effect of having too much money in the economy chasing too few goods.

34 The current rate that the UK aims for is 2%, but other monetary authorities such as the European Central Bank view 2% as a ceiling and consider that rates below 2% are acceptable. Many economists think a little inflation is a good thing, and most economists think high rates of inflation, say over 8–10%, are a major problem.

35 There are other aspects to monetary policy, such as quantitative easing. There are also fiscal policy and supply-side approaches to reach economics objectives.

36 Changes in interest rates are considered to be demand-side policies, but they do have supply-side impact. This is because the interest rate changes impact upon the demand side more quickly and more significantly.

37 The result would be no change in output or the price level. A shift to the right in *AS* where *AD* crosses at the horizontal part of *AS* would have no impact on the economy — except to increase the amount of spare capacity.

38 On the demand side, there are fiscal and monetary policies; and on the supply side, supply-side policies. There are other macroeconomic policies, but you do not need to know them for Unit 2.

39 Contractionary fiscal policy can involve an increase in tax or a cut in government spending — or both.

40 If heavy borrowing pushes up interest rates, this tends to affect lower-income groups disproportionately more because lower-income groups tend to have larger levels of debt relative to income.

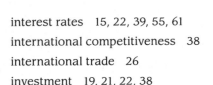

Edexcel AS Economics

⌇ PHILIP ALLAN

STUDENT UNIT GUIDES | NEW EDITIONS

- Clear revision guidance
- Examiner advice
- Sample questions and answers

Don't miss out on the best grades in all your A-level subjects.

There are Student Unit Guides for:

Accounting (AQA)

Biology (AQA, CCEA, Edexcel, OCR)

Business Studies (AQA, Edexcel, OCR)

Chemistry (AQA, Edexcel, OCR (A), OCR (B) (Salters))

Critical Thinking (OCR)

Economics (AQA, Edexcel, OCR)

Geography (AQA, Edexcel, OCR, WJEC)

Government & Politics (AQA, Edexcel)

History (CCEA, Edexcel, OCR)

Law (AQA, OCR)

Mathematics (AQA, Edexcel, OCR)

Media Studies (AQA)

Physical Education (AQA, Edexcel, OCR)

Physics (Edexcel, OCR)

Psychology (AQA (A), AQA (B), Edexcel, OCR)

Sociology (AQA, OCR)

Visit **www.philipallan.co.uk** for the full list of unit guides and to order online, or telephone our Customer Services Department on **01235 827827**